SAKA

MATT AND TOM OLDFIELD

ULTIMATE FOOTBALL HEROES

SAKA

FROM THE PLAYGROUND TO THE PITCH

DINO

First published by Dino Books in 2022,
an imprint of Bonnier Books UK,
4th Floor, Victoria House, Bloomsbury Square, London WC1B 4DA
Owned by Bonnier Books,
Sveavägen 56, Stockholm, Sweden

@UFHbooks
@footieheroesbks
www.heroesfootball.com
www.bonnierbooks.co.uk

Text © Matt Oldfield 2022

Design by www.envydesign.co.uk

Paperback ISBN: 978 1 78946 480 1
E-book ISBN: 978 1 78946 481 8

British Library cataloguing-in-publication data:
A catalogue record for this book is available from the British Library.

Printed and bound in Great Britain by Clays Ltd, Elcograf S.p.A.

1 3 5 7 9 10 8 6 4 2

For all readers,
young and old(er)

Matt Oldfield is an accomplished writer and the editor-in-chief of football review site Of Pitch & Page. Tom Oldfield is a freelance sports writer and the author of biographies on Cristiano Ronaldo, Arsène Wenger and Rafael Nadal.

Cover illustration by Dan Leydon.
To learn more about Dan visit danleydon.com
To purchase his artwork visit etsy.com/shop/footynews
Or just follow him on Twitter @danleydon

TABLE OF CONTENTS

ACKNOWLEDGEMENTS

First of all, I'd like to thank everyone at Bonnier
Books UK for supporting me throughout and for
running the ever-expanding UFH ship so smoothly.
Writing stories for the next generation of football fans
is both an honour and a pleasure. Thanks also to my
agent, Nick Walters, for helping to keep my dream
job going, year after year.

Next up, an extra big cheer for all the teachers,
booksellers and librarians who have championed these
books, and, of course, for the readers. The success
of this series is truly down to you.

Okay, onto friends and family. I wouldn't be writing
this series if it wasn't for my brother Tom. I owe him

so much and I'm very grateful for his belief in me as an author. I'm also very grateful to the rest of my family, especially Mel, Noah, Nico, and of course Mum and Dad. To my parents, I owe my biggest passions: football and books. They're a real inspiration for everything I do.

Pang, Will, Mills, Doug, Naomi, John, Charlie, Sam, Katy, Ben, Karen, Ana (and anyone else I forgot) – thanks for all the love and laughs, but sorry, no I won't be getting 'a real job' anytime soon!

And finally, I couldn't have done any of this without Iona's encouragement and understanding. Much love to you.

CHAPTER 1

ENGLAND'S NEW EURO 2020 HERO

22 June 2021, Wembley Stadium

As Harry Kane led the England team out onto the pitch, there was a crowd of nearly 20,000 excited fans waiting for them. After two years of playing in empty stadiums due to the COVID-19 pandemic, the roar sounded so good.

Come on England, come on England!

Most of the line-up had already experienced the electric Wembley atmosphere after featuring in their first two matches at Euro 2020 – a 1–0 win over Croatia, followed by a disappointing 0–0 draw with Scotland. But for their final must-win group game

against the Czech Republic, the England manager
Gareth Southgate had made some changes in attack.
Jack Grealish for Mason Mount was a swap that most
people were expecting, but the replacement of Phil
Foden on the right wing was much more of a surprise.
Not with Marcus Rashford, or Jadon Sancho, but with
Bukayo Saka!

At the age of only nineteen, Arsenal's rising star was
about to represent England in a major tournament!
Just being named in England's Euro 2020 squad
had been a lovely surprise, but to be selected in the
starting line-up – it was beyond Bukayo's wildest
dreams.

As he stood and sang the national anthem, though,
Bukayo didn't look nervous or worried at all. Why
should he have been, though? He had worked so hard
for this opportunity, ever since signing for Arsenal at
the age of seven. At the Euros, he had been watching,
waiting and learning as much as possible from the
senior England players every day in training. He had
successfully impressed Southgate with his talent and
attitude, and now, it was time to give his all on the

pitch for his country.

'Let's win this!' Kyle Walker cheered as the anthem
ended. With all his experience, he was the perfect
player for Bukayo to have behind him on the right
side for England. Although he often played on the
left for Arsenal, either in defence or midfield, Bukayo
had the speed, skill, intelligence and energy to play in
almost any position. That's why his managers loved
him so much – he was such a useful footballer to have
around.

As well as his work-rate, there was one other
reason why Bukayo was the right man for the job: he
had humiliated the Czech left-back, Jan Bořil, once
before in the Europa League quarter-final. That night,
Arsenal's young winger had grabbed a goal and an
assist, while the Slavia Prague defender was taken off
at half-time.

So, could Bukayo embarrass Bořil again? He was
involved in the game almost straight away, as he
calmly chested the ball down and played a simple pass
back to Kyle. It was a good start, but now he needed
to push forward and attack.

'Just do what you do at Arsenal,' Southgate had told him in the dressing room. 'Play with confidence and freedom, and enjoy yourself.'

Yes, Boss! In the eleventh minute, Bukayo dropped deep to collect the ball off Kyle, and then spun and dribbled forward at speed, leaving the Czech midfielders trailing behind him. After crossing the halfway line, he passed the ball to Kalvin Phillips, but Bukayo didn't stop there. No, he kept on running into the box for the one-two.

When the return pass arrived, Bukayo twisted and turned away from two defenders and delivered a deep cross to the back post, but it was too high for Harry. Eventually, it came out to Jack on the left wing, who curled in another cross. As the ball floated across the six-yard box, Bukayo made his move, from the right to the middle. He leapt up high to meet it, but unfortunately, it flew just over his head. But there was no need to worry; Raheem Sterling was right behind him and he nodded the ball into the net. *1–0!* Hurray, England were winning at Wembley!

'Come on!' Bukayo cried out, punching the air with

passion. With the fans cheering wildly, he rushed over to celebrate with his teammates. He hadn't scored the goal himself, but he had played an important part in setting it up. On his way back for the restart, he stopped to remove his underlayer. It was too hot to wear two shirts; he was on fire!

England had the goal they needed, but Bukayo wanted more. Every time he got the ball, his first thought was, 'Attack!' And so he dribbled forward again and again, forcing Bořil to back away in fear. Although he couldn't quite find the killer final pass to Harry or Raheem, Bukayo was causing all kinds of problems for the Czech defence.

'Unlucky, keep going!' Southgate clapped and cheered on the sidelines.

Yes, Boss! Bukayo showed more of the same fearlessness in the second half. As he received the ball with his back to goal, he had a Czech player right behind him, but he used his strength to hold him off and then chipped a brilliant pass through to Harry.

'What a ball!' the England fans roared. Bukayo was fast becoming one of their favourite players.

As the game went on, Bořil grew more and more frustrated by his impressive opponent. Every time he tried to close him down, Bukayo somehow managed to wriggle away until eventually, the defender tripped him up and dragged him to the floor. Yellow card! Oh dear, Bořil was having another bad day against Bukayo.

For all his attacking flair, Bukayo was also happy to chase back and do his defensive duties when needed. As a left-back at Arsenal, he had learned to track his marker and be in the right position to make the block.

'Nice one, mate!' Kyle shouted as he cleared the ball away upfield.

After eighty-four amazing minutes, Bukayo's dream Euro 2020 debut came to an end. As he walked off, all the England fans rose to their feet to clap for their new national hero.

'Well played, bro,' said Marcus and Jadon, giving him high-fives as he left the field.

'Wow, what a performance!' said Southgate on the touchline, giving him a great big hug.

At last, Bukayo allowed his focus to drop and a

smile to spread across his face. Yes, he had certainly made the most of his chance to shine at Euro 2020.

England held on to win 1–0 and finish top of Group D. Next up, in the Round of 16, they would face their old enemies Germany, but that could wait. For now, all everyone was talking about was the man of the match: Bukayo! The boy from Ealing, West London, had just burst onto the scene as England's new superstar. What an exciting future he had ahead of him.

CHAPTER 2

EARLY KICKS
IN EALING

'Where is he? He's LATE!'

While they waited impatiently for their father to get home from work, Bukayo and his older brother Yomi did the only thing they could do: they practised inside, kicking a balloon up in the air between them. It just wasn't the same, though. Nothing compared to the real thing, and that's why they needed their father to hurry up and get home – so that they could go outside and play a proper game with him!

Yomi Senior had fallen in love with football long before he moved to England from Nigeria, but with the chance to watch the Premier League on TV every week, his passion for the sport had grown stronger and stronger. Although the Sakas lived in Ealing, West London, he didn't support Chelsea, or Tottenham, or Arsenal. No, instead he supported Newcastle United. Why them? Because his favourite player was their striker, Alan Shearer. By 2005, Shearer's career was coming to an end, 'but you should have seen him when he was younger,' he often told his boys. 'What a superstar he was!'

There was one thing, though, that Yomi Senior loved even more than watching and talking about football, and that was playing it. And being able to play the beautiful game with his sons was exactly that – beautiful. He enjoyed every minute of it, after work and especially at the weekends.

'Quick, he's coming!' Yomi Jr called out suddenly.

Together, the brothers watched through the window with great excitement as at last their father approached their house. As soon as he was through the front door, he dropped his work bag and hugged his sons.

'Sorry boys, Shearer's back! Right, are you ready for a quick game?'

'Yayyyyyy!'

Grabbing the ball from the cupboard, Yomi Sr led his sons outside and onto the pitch. In reality, their garden was just a small square of grass, but through the young boys' eyes, it was as wonderful and important as any big football stadium.

'Okay, you're the youngest Bukayo, so you can start with the ball today,' their dad decided.

Yes, Yomi Jr was older, but his competitive younger brother was catching up quickly. Each and every day, Bukayo's left foot was growing more powerful and his football skills were improving: his ball control, passing, dribbling, shooting. He was determined to become the best footballer in the family as soon as possible.

Bukayo's name meant 'adds to happiness' in Yoruba, one of Nigeria's main languages, and most of the time, he was a very happy four-year-old boy. If he was losing on the family football pitch, however, his smile soon disappeared.

'Can we go inside now? I'm hungry!' Yomi Jr complained after a while.

Bukayo shook his head and clenched his fists. It was

easy for his brother to say that; he was winning. 'No, we haven't finished the game yet.'

'Come on, son, your brother's right. It's getting dark – we can carry on tomorrow.'

'No!'

Sometimes, the two Yomis managed to persuade him to stop, but usually, they agreed to play on until Bukayo was the winner. It was easier for everyone that way.

'Cool, can we go inside and eat now?' his brother asked.

'Yesssssssss!' he replied, with a big smile back on his face.

For Bukayo, those garden games were just the beginning. Once he got a bit older, he was allowed to go out and play on his own on the green in front of their house. Much better; now he had more space and there was no-one there to stop him. Most nights, he would be out there for hours, practising the same ball skills again and again until bedtime.

'He's certainly got the dedication to be a professional player one day,' Yomi said to his wife,

Adenike, as they watched their hard-working son through the window.

Yes, but what about the talent? The Sakas would have to wait and see, but the next step was finding Bukayo a first football team.

CHAPTER 3

TOP LONDON CLUBS CALLING!

Bukayo's first football club turned out to be a team called Greenford Celtic, who played in the local Harrow Youth League. He joined at the age of seven, but he didn't stay there long. That wasn't because he didn't enjoy it or he wasn't good enough, though. No, it was the exact opposite; he was *too* good!

After a few man-of-the-match performances full of goals and assists, word quickly spread about Ealing's exciting new forward. The kid was strong, skilful, super-speedy, and he had a lethal left foot – what more could you want from a young footballer? Suddenly, all of London's biggest football clubs were sending scouts to watch him play.

Wow, Bukayo was a boy in high demand! He decided to start off at the Watford development centre, where his brother Yomi was also training. He liked it there because the club's youth coaches were friendly and the training sessions were fun, but did Bukayo have the special talent to go even higher? You see, Watford had recently been relegated to the Championship, and there were top Premier League teams chasing him...

Including Chelsea. Since Russian billionaire Roman Abramovich bought the club in 2003, The Blues had won the FA Cup once, the League Cup twice, and the Premier League title twice as well. That was a lot of top trophies for one team to win, and their squad was full of superstars, like John Terry, Frank Lampard and Didier Drogba.

So, when Chelsea asked Bukayo if he would be interested in coming along for a trial, he said, 'Yes please!' straight away. Their brand-new academy complex was absolutely amazing, but the only problem was that it was based in Surrey, nearly thirty miles away from the Saka family home. Hmm, that would be a very long and boring journey to make two or three times every week.

Well if not them, then what about Tottenham? Spurs definitely didn't have as much money or as many trophies as Chelsea, but they were still a top Premier League club and their new manager Harry Redknapp was building a brilliant team with talented young British players like Gareth Bale, Tom Huddlestone and Aaron Lennon.

Maybe Bukayo could be next! When the coaches at the Tottenham academy invited him to visit, his parents encouraged him to go. 'It's important for you to try different clubs and decide which one you like best,' his dad told him. So, off they drove from West London to North London for some training sessions at Spurs Lodge. Bukayo enjoyed his short time there, but he had one more option to think about:

Arsenal. Although the glory years of Thierry Henry and Dennis Bergkamp were over, The Gunners were still one of England and Europe's biggest clubs. Their team now featured new stars like Cesc Fàbregas, Emmanuel Adebayor and Robin van Persie, and every season, they competed for all the top trophies, including the Champions League.

At Arsenal, it wasn't just about winning, though. Under legendary manager Arsène Wenger, the team was famous for playing a beautiful style of football, with lots of flowing passing moves from defence to attack. Did Bukayo like the sound of that? Oh yes he did! So, off he drove with his dad, again from West London to North London again, this time to visit Arsenal's youth training centre in Hale End.

After spending time at all three academies, Bukayo had a choice to make. Which of London's biggest football clubs was he going to play for: Chelsea, Tottenham or Arsenal? It seemed like a massive decision for a seven-year-old, so Bukayo's parents tried to keep things as relaxed and simple as possible for their son.

'Don't worry, this is not forever!' they reassured him. 'Don't think about the future; just think about fun because that's what football's all about at your age. Which academy's training sessions did you enjoy the most?'

CHAPTER 4

ARSENAL ALL THE WAY!

For Bukayo, the answer to that question was easy: Arsenal all the way!

They were his favourite team to watch on TV because they always made football look so elegant and entertaining. And as he had experienced for himself during his visit to the academy, that style of play wasn't just a Premier League thing; it was the Arsenal way, taught from the top all the way down to the Under-8s.

'And that's the way I want to play too!' Bukayo told his parents at the dinner table.

'Arsenal it is, then!' his dad declared happily.

Yomi Sr had stayed quiet while his son made up his

mind, but he was delighted with his final decision. Although he was a Newcastle fan, he had always liked Arsenal too, and he had a lot of respect and admiration for Wenger as a manager. The Frenchman taught his teams to play beautiful football and he believed in bringing through young players and giving them a chance. So yes, Bukayo's dad was sure that his son would be in very safe hands at Hale End. Not only had he seen that the coaching was excellent, but he knew that there was a clear path between the Arsenal academy and the first team, which many players had taken in recent years:

Fàbregas,

Johan Djourou,

Nicklas Bendtner,

Wojciech Szczęsny,

Kieran Gibbs...

...and most exciting of all, young English midfielder Jack Wilshere. At the age of only sixteen, he was already playing for Arsenal in the Premier League, and if he could do it, then why couldn't Bukayo follow in his footsteps one day? That was the ultimate goal for

Bukayo, but first he had a long, hard road ahead of him, full of ups and downs and frustrating car journeys with his dad.

'How much further? Why aren't we moving? I'm going to be late!'

On a good day, the drive to training, from Ealing to Walthamstow, took them less than an hour, but it was often a lot longer than that if there were roadworks and they got stuck in bad traffic. Some nights, they spent over three hours in the car together, but for Bukayo, it was all worth it for the proud feeling of playing for Arsenal.

Bukayo enjoyed every minute of the training sessions, and the matches too. This was proper, serious football now, which meant lots of fun, but also lots of hard work, especially as he had some catching up to do. Bukayo's new teammates at Hale End were already so talented with the ball at their feet, and that really spurred him on to keep learning and improving aspects of his own game, like his first touch, his heading, and his right foot.

And as well as working on his weaknesses, Bukayo

also worked on his strengths. He had always thought of himself as a pretty good dribbler, but at the Arsenal academy, they helped him to take his wizardry to the next level. He learned to take a slightly heavier touch to draw the defender towards him, and then when they tried to tackle him, he used his speed and skill to skip straight past them.

'That's it – well played, Bukayo!'

By putting in 100 per cent effort and listening carefully to his coaches, he was getting better and better every week. Once upon a time, he had been determined to become the best footballer in his family, but now Bukayo was aiming a lot higher than that. He wanted to become the best footballer in the whole Arsenal academy, 'the next Jack Wilshere' who made it all the way from the Under-9s to the first team. He knew that less than 1 per cent of the youngsters at the academy achieved that aim, but that wasn't going to stop him from trying his hardest.

'I can do this!' Bukayo kept telling himself.

While his parents wanted him to get a good education as well, they were always supportive of his professional football dream. When he was eight years old, his dad took him to Old Trafford to see his beloved Newcastle play away at Manchester United, and what a memorable day it was for young Bukayo. When the two teams walked out of the tunnel, he was blown away by the sound of over 70,000 supporters all singing together. Wow, the atmosphere was out of this world!

'It must be so amazing to be one of those players out on the pitch,' Bukayo thought to himself.

The experience made him even more sure about what he wanted to be when he was older: a Premier League superstar. But not for Newcastle or Manchester United – no, Bukayo was Arsenal all the way!

CHAPTER 5

GREENFORD HIGH'S HUMBLE HERO

Although Bukayo was Arsenal all the way, that didn't stop him from shining for his school teams too. First, he helped Edward Betham Primary to win the Ealing Peal Shield two years in a row, and then he moved on to Greenford High, where the football coach spotted his unique talent straight away.

Dipesh Patel had worked with lots of very promising academy players before, including Bukayo's older brother Yomi, but there was something extra special about this kid. Was it his speed or his skill? Both were excellent, but no – it was actually Bukayo's football intelligence and his humble attitude that impressed Patel the most. Even though he was a

Tottenham fan, Patel had to admit that the Arsenal youngster was a future superstar.

In all his years as a coach, he had never seen an eleven-year-old who could read the game so well and make the right decisions so often. Bukayo always seemed to know where to move to find space and then what to do next – pass, cross, dribble or shoot. Again and again, he created game-changing moments for Greenford.

'Wow, that was magic, mate!' his teammates called out as they celebrated another great goal. 'What would we do without you?'

But for all Bukayo's brilliance, he never behaved like an arrogant superstar. No, he was far too polite and modest for that, and too calm to get carried away. Even when his school coach sometimes took him off at half-time to give their opponents a bit of a chance, Bukayo just did what he was told and never complained. Winning wasn't about him; it was always about the team, and everyone working hard together.

'Well done, Bukayo – sorry, those poor defenders needed a break from you!'

In Bukayo's first year at the school, Greenford made it all the way to the final of the Ealing Borough Trophy. His teammates were counting on him to be their matchwinner yet again, but for once, his football brain failed him. With the pressure on, he missed goalscoring chance after chance and Greenford ended up losing the match.

Nooooooo! At the final whistle, Bukayo was furious with himself and with the whole world. In the biggest match of the year, why had he played so badly? He was so much better than that! He was supposed to be the star of the school team and it felt like it was all his fault.

'I'm never playing football again!' he told his manager angrily.

But of course, Bukayo didn't really give up on the game he loved. No, once he had calmed down and the disappointment had faded, he bounced back better than ever. As well as improving his own performances, he also helped raise the level of the other players around him. Together, their school team became unbeatable! The next year, Greenford made it back to the Ealing Borough Trophy final, and this time they won it, along with the Middlesex Cup too.

'Yes, we did it – County Champions!' Bukayo cheered as he lifted his second school trophy with all his teammates.

So, what else could Greenford High's humble hero achieve? With his amazing athleticism, he had the potential to be great at any sport. His PE teacher Mark Harvey tried to persuade him to join the school basketball team as well, but in the end, the youngster decided to stick to football.

Besides, Bukayo didn't have time for two sports because he also had hours of schoolwork to do. Yes, he was on track to become a top professional footballer, but his parents wanted him to get good GCSE grades first. Yomi and Adenike always encouraged their sons to play the game they loved and they drove them across London for training every week – Bukayo to Arsenal, and Yomi Jr to Watford. But they believed that education was also very important.

As he got older, Bukayo had to miss quite a lot of

classes because he was away playing for the Arsenal academy, but he made sure that his school grades never slipped. Whether he did it at home or in the car while his dad drove him to training, Bukayo always did his work, and he was such a respectful, responsible boy that his teachers were always happy to give him extra help after school.

All that studying for the exams was worth it in the end. When he received his GCSE results, Bukayo was delighted. He had performed brilliantly in all seven subjects, getting the top grade in four of them, including Business Studies and, of course, PE.

'Congratulations, son – we're so proud of you!' his parents praised him. 'Now, you're free to focus fully on your football.'

CHAPTER 6

WORKING HARD
AT HALE END

Whether he was at school or at Hale End, Bukayo
was always working hard to become the best that he
could be. Every time he arrived at Arsenal training, he
looked up at the huge picture of Wilshere on the wall,
and told himself, 'I can make it to the first team too –
there's a pathway.'

While Bukayo always enjoyed playing football
for Arsenal, life at the academy wasn't easy. There
were so many talented young players at the club but
they couldn't all get to the top, and so every year,
some of them were sadly released. Most found other
football teams to move to, but others stopped playing
completely.

Fortunately for him, Bukayo was never one of the ones let go, but as he progressed through the age groups at Arsenal, things got more and more competitive. All it took was a few poor performances or an injury, and you could lose your place in the team forever. Bukayo just had to keep doing his best, in each and every training session and match to ensure that never happened.

Bukayo rarely had a bad game, but he did go through some injury problems. After an early growth spurt, he started getting pains in his heels and then in his knees, and they wouldn't go away. The Arsenal physios assured him that it was normal and he just needed to be patient, but that was probably the hardest thing for a young aspiring footballer to hear.

'How long until I can play again without it hurting?' Bukayo kept asking every week. Argghh, it was so frustrating; he just wanted to get back on the pitch as soon as possible!

Eventually, Bukayo's growing pains did go away, but there were further challenges ahead. As a young teenager he was one of the tallest and strongest players in his team, and that gave him an extra edge on the football pitch. Again and again, he used his superior speed and power to burst past defenders and score.

'But what about when the other kids catch up?' some of the Arsenal youth coaches began to wonder. 'And what about when he's playing against adults – if he's not bigger than his opponents, will Bukayo still be as good?'

The answer, of course, was yes! As a footballer, he had so much more than just speed and strength; he also had skill, intelligence, and perhaps most importantly of all, incredible determination. Through hard work and dedication, Bukayo was capable of overcoming any obstacle in his path.

'What can I do to become a better player?' Bukayo asked himself that question constantly, whether he was doing a training drill at Hale End or watching football on TV at home with his dad. While Yomi had enjoyed games as a fan, his youngest son observed them as a student.

What movements did the wingers make to find

space on the pitch?

Did they stay out wide, drift into the middle, or even swap wings?

How many times did they check over their shoulder before they got the ball?

How often did they try to dribble past the defenders, and how often did they cut inside for the cross?

And how did they decide what to do so quickly and under so much pressure?

There was so much for Bukayo to learn from his football heroes. His favourite player of all time was Arsenal legend Thierry Henry, but Alexis Sánchez, Arsenal's Number Seven, was the one he loved to watch the most in the modern first team. With the ball at his feet, the Chilean forward was so entertaining and Bukayo was lucky enough to see him play up close lots of times at the Emirates Stadium.

'Woah, did you see that skill?!' he kept crying out until eventually the other academy players next to him told him to shut up. After that, Bukayo did stay quiet, but he didn't stop admiring the way that Alexis played. Instead in training, he practised and practised until he mastered his signature move, the 'Sanchez roll' to dribble past the defender. In fact, he wanted to be like his hero so much that for a while he even wore the same football boots as him.

'Look everyone, Alexis is in the building!' Bukayo's teammates teased him. 'Shouldn't you be training with the first team, mate?'

As well as watching matches live and on TV, Bukayo also liked to watch lots of old highlights on YouTube. He never got tired of seeing Henry's greatest goals for Arsenal, but to get himself pumped up before games, he preferred skills videos, usually starring three of football's most amazing magicians: Lionel Messi, Neymar Jr, and Cristiano Ronaldo. Wow, talk about unbelievable tekkers!

Watching those wizards made Bukayo feel happy and it also got him in the mood to create some magic of his own. He was on fire at the Arsenal academy and with each star performance, he was getting closer and closer to the first team. In 2017, he helped the Under-

16s to lift the Liam Brady Cup, scoring goals against Bayern Munich and Manchester United. At the end of the season, his coach had great news for him: Bukayo would be moving up to the Under-18s.

'Congratulations!' Yomi cheered on the long drive home. 'But don't get carried away, son; remember, you're not a Premier League superstar yet.'

'Thanks, yes I know that!' Bukayo laughed and rolled his eyes. It was always good to have his dad there to keep him humble and grounded, especially now that he was a rising star, for Arsenal and for England.

Bukayo had received his first call-up to play for his country when he was only fourteen years old, in an Under-16s friendly match against the USA at St George's Park. Wow, what an honour! Although he was very proud of his Nigerian heritage, West London had always been his home. As a little boy practising in his garden in Ealing, he had dreamed of playing football for England, and amazingly, that dream was already coming true.

For the first half, Bukayo sat on the subs bench with his Arsenal teammate, Xavier Amaechi, watching and waiting. At last, after sixty minutes, their big moment arrived. Xavier came on to play on the right wing, and Bukayo came on to play on the left, but not on the wing. No, instead he was at left-back.

While Arsenal normally put him in a more attacking role, Bukayo was happy to play in any position for England. Plus, the advantage of being in defence was that he was able to use his speed and power to burst forward from deep. Although he didn't score on his debut, he did in his second game two days later.

GOAL! Whether he was playing for club or country, at left back or left wing, Bukayo was proving to be simply unstoppable.

CHAPTER 7

AWESOME FOR THE ARSENAL UNDER-18S

Every summer, Bukayo set himself new targets for the season ahead: number of goals, number of assists, and number of trophies. So, what was he hoping for in 2017–18? Well, now that he was part of the Arsenal Under-18s, there were two big trophies up for grabs: the U18 Premier League South and the FA Youth Cup. Lifting one would be brilliant, but as always, Bukayo was aiming high.

'Come on, we can win them both this year!' he told his new teammates confidently.

That wasn't going to be easy for the young Gunners, though. Their London rivals Chelsea had been crowned Premier League South champions for the last three seasons in a row, while Arsenal hadn't won the FA Youth Cup since Wilshere's team back in 2009.

Could the current Under-18s become the club's next golden generation? Of course, they could! Under manager Kwame Ampadu, the team looked strong at the back and really exciting in attack. Although their star man Emile Smith Rowe was now mostly playing for the Under-23s, they had found an excellent replacement on the left wing: Bukayo! At first, U18s football felt like a big step-up to him, but with each game he played, he got better and better.

On his second start in the league against Reading, Bukayo battled for the ball, dribbled forward, and played a clever pass across to striker Tyreece John-Jules, who scored to make it 3–0.

Against Southampton, Bukayo raced up the left wing and whipped in a beautiful cross for defender Daniel Ballard to head in. Then moments later, he scored a great goal of his own, this time from the right. As the ball came to him, he faked to pass down the line, but instead he cut inside on his left foot and fired a curling shot into the bottom corner. *5–1!*

Goooooooooooooooooooaaaaaaaaaaaaaaaalllllllllllll lllllllllll!!!!!!!!!!!!!!!!!!!

Bukayo played it cool as he high-fived his teammates, but on the inside, he was delighted with his goal. He was already off the mark for the Under-18s and he'd only just turned sixteen!

Soon, it was time for Arsenal's biggest game of the season so far: the North London derby against Tottenham. From his first day at the club at the age of seven, Bukayo had been told about the importance of this particular fixture. And so, like all true heroes, he saved his best performance for the biggest game.

In the eighteenth minute, Bukayo pounced on a Spurs mistake to give the young Gunners the lead, and from there, it was Arsenal all the way.

Trae Coyle scored the second,

Xavier scored the third,

And Bukayo added a fourth before half-time with a cool first-time finish.

Goooooooooooooooooooaaaaaaaaaaaaaaaalllllllllllll lllllllllll!!!!!!!!!!!!!!!!!!!

Following a quick fist pump, he ran over to thank his right-back Vontae Daley-Campbell for the assist. Arsenal's young hero was still as humble as ever.

By the final whistle, they had won 6–0 – hurray, North London was red! With another win over Swansea City, Bukayo and the Under-18s moved up to second place in the U18 Premier League, six points behind leaders Chelsea.

After that, Arsenal's young stars switched their focus to the FA Youth Cup for a while. In the third round, Xavier scored both goals as they beat Sheffield Wednesday, but in the fourth round, the young Gunners were just minutes away from losing to Liverpool and going out of the competition.

Nooooo – Bukayo wasn't going to let that happen. With Emile back for the FA Youth Cup, he had started on the bench, but his manager brought him on midway through the second half to try and change the game.

'Right, I can do this,' Bukayo told himself as he sprinted onto the pitch. He was ready to be Arsenal's super sub.

As the ball came to him, he flicked it over the defender's head and chased after it. He had the speed and strength to get there first and carry the ball into the penalty area, but what next – cross or shoot? The angle looked really tight, but with a whip of his left foot, Bukayo fired a shot over the keeper and into the net. *2–2!*

Goooooooooooooooooooooaaaaaaaaaaaaaaaaallllllllllllll llllllllllllll!!!!!!!!!!!!!!!!!!!!

'Yes, you hero!' Emile cried out, giving his teammate a huge hug.

In extra-time, Bukayo saved the day for Arsenal again. Racing onto Emile's defence-splitting pass, he shrugged off the Liverpool centre-back and then calmly crossed the ball to Tyreece, who scored the winning goal. Phew, thanks to their awesome super sub, Arsenal were still in the competition!

After that lucky escape against Liverpool, the young Gunners cruised their way through to the FA Youth Cup final, past Middlesbrough, Colchester, and then Blackpool in the semis. In the final, Arsenal faced their U18 Premier League South rivals Chelsea. Their team was packed with such talented young players:

Marc Guéhi, Reece James and Tariq Lamptey in defence,

Billy Gilmour and Conor Gallagher in midfield,

And George McEachran and Callum Hudson-Odoi in attack.

Arsenal, however, were determined to show no fear. Why should they? They had lots of future superstars of their own!

In the first leg away at Stamford Bridge, Emile set up Xavier to score the opening goal, but in the second half, Chelsea came storming back, scoring three times in the last twenty-five minutes. Sadly, it was their striker, Daishawn Redan, who was the super sub this time, not Bukayo. He could only watch as the goals went in, and wish he'd changed the game.

Oh well, at least there was a second leg. Back at the Emirates, Bukayo was bumped up to the Arsenal starting line-up, but he struggled to make an impact. Although he ran and ran all game long, Chelsea were just too good for them. The Blues thrashed the Gunners 4–0 to win the FA Youth Cup for the fifth year in a row and complete the Under-18s league and cup double.

At the final whistle, Bukayo felt gutted as he shook hands with his opponents, but at the same time, he knew that he had done his best for his team, just like he had all season. He was still learning and he was still only sixteen. There was always next year's FA Youth Cup, when Bukayo would be older, wiser, and hopefully, even more awesome for Arsenal.

CHAPTER 8

EURO 2017 WITH THE ENGLAND UNDER-17S

Although he hadn't managed to win a trophy with the Arsenal Under-18s, Bukayo felt pleased with his overall progress. Twenty-one games, eight goals and five assists – those were really good numbers for his first season at that level, and they were only going to get better.

It wasn't holiday time yet, though. First, Bukayo would have one more go at glory with the England Under-17s at the 2017 UEFA European Championships.

In previous years, the tournament had involved fun trips to Azerbaijan and Croatia, but this time, England were hosting the Euros themselves. Instead of matches at Wembley or the Emirates or Old Trafford, however, they would be playing at stadiums in Walsall, Chesterfield, and Rotherham. There probably wouldn't be many supporters watching their matches at 3pm on a Monday anyway, but Bukayo didn't mind at all. He couldn't wait to represent his country at such a major tournament, and his whole family would be there to cheer him on.

For England's first game against Israel, the manager Steve Cooper named him in the starting line-up, alongside his academy teammates Xavier, Tyreece and Vontae. It was like Arsenal all over again, only with one major twist – Bukayo would be playing on the right wing, rather than the left.

No problem! He had the skill, speed and intelligence to shine in any position. In the twenty-eighth minute, Bukayo got the ball and weaved his way into the box until eventually a defender fouled him. Penalty! Tommy Doyle scored it to give England the lead.

'Get in!' Bukayo cheered with pride at the part he had played in the goal.

In the second half, Sampson asked him to switch positions again, this time to left-back. There, Bukayo defended well, while also pushing forward to join the attack at every opportunity. What a useful player he was to have!

Left-back was where Bukayo stayed as England beat Italy to make it through the group stage, but for the quarter-final against Norway, his manager gave him another new role: left wing-back.

Great, even better! With his amazing energy, Bukayo could get up and down the pitch all game long. Early in the second half, he dribbled forward past one defender and then poked a great pass through to Bobby Duncan. Bobby's cross found Xavier in space in the middle, and he calmly side-footed the ball into the bottom corner. *2–0!* It was an excellent team goal, sending England on their way to the Euro semi-finals.

Up next: the Netherlands. Their tricky winger Crysencio Summerville was a really dangerous opponent, but with the senior England manager Gareth Southgate watching, Bukayo battled hard and stopped him from scoring. He didn't just sit back and defend all game, though – no, he also sprinted forward to help the attack as much as possible.

'I'm here!' he called out, making overlapping runs past the winger, Rayhaan Tulloch.

If England were going to score, it looked like the goal would certainly come from the left. First, Bukayo fired a shot just over the bar, and then just before half-time, he slid a brilliant ball across the six-yard box. Surely, one of his England teammates would tap it in? But no, Bobby couldn't quite reach it, and neither could Arvin Appiah at the back post. So close! Bukayo threw his hands to his head in disappointment. His assist definitely deserved a goal!

At the full-time whistle, however, neither team had scored, and so the semi-final went to a penalty shoot-out. So, who was brave enough to step up for England? Some players found it too much pressure, but Bukayo put his hand up straight away to take one. First, however, he needed some physio treatment for the cramp in his legs.

By the time Bukayo walked forward from the halfway line, the pressure had grown even greater because the first five penalties had all been scored. Uh-oh, was he going to be the first one to miss?

No, Bukayo was fearless and well-prepared. After a short run-up, he coolly placed the ball low into the bottom corner. *GOAL!* It was a perfect penalty but he didn't celebrate at all – no punch of the air, no hint of a smile. Both could wait until his team had won.

Sadly, that joyful moment didn't arrive. In the end, the shoot-out went all the way to sudden death. Quinten Timber scored for the Netherlands, while Folarin Balogun's spot-kick was saved. *Noooo*, England had been knocked out of the Euros!

As some of his teammates sank to their knees in despair, Bukayo stood there frozen in deep disappointment. First the FA Youth Cup and the U18 Premier League title with Arsenal, and now this with England – yet another nearly moment! It was gutting to get so close to reaching the Euros final, and Bukayo was beginning to wonder if he would ever win a trophy again.

'Look, I know it feels painful right now, but you should all be really proud of the way you've played throughout the tournament,' Cooper tried to comfort his players afterwards. 'We didn't deserve to lose that game, and together, we're going to bounce back better than ever, okay?'

Moments later, there was a knock on the dressing room door and in walked an unexpected visitor…

'I'm sorry the result didn't go your way tonight,' Southgate said, 'but I thought you all performed really well, like a proper England team. So keep your heads up and keep going – you're on the right path.'

With those positive words in his head, Bukayo didn't stay downhearted for long. He was still in the early stages of his international career, and hopefully he would have plenty more chances in the future to win trophies for England.

CHAPTER 9

LEARNING FROM LJUNGBERG

Back at Hale End, there was big news waiting for Bukayo. Despite still being sixteen years old, the academy coaches had decided that he was ready to take the next step. For the 2018–19 season, he was moving up to the Arsenal Under-23s!

Wow, Bukayo couldn't wait. Not only would he be playing alongside old friends like Xavier, Tyreece and Emile, but he would also have the chance to learn from an absolute club legend. Freddie Ljungberg had been a key part of the amazing Arsenal team that won two Premier League titles and three FA Cups between 2001 and 2005. During those glory years, the Swedish midfielder had set up lots of goals for Henry and

Bergkamp, and now, he was using his experience to coach Arsenal's stars of the future.

Lucky Bukayo! He had first worked with Ljungberg in the Under-15s, and he was excited to link up with him again. As a former winger himself, Freddie had lots of top tips to offer, and Bukayo was going to need lots of guidance to help him adapt to playing at a higher level, where the football would be faster and the defenders would be stronger.

'Don't worry, as long as you keep working hard, you're going to be great,' his new manager assured him. He believed in Bukayo and knew that he had the ability and mentality to rise to the challenge. Sometimes, young players just needed a push in order to reach their full potential.

For the first few games of the Premier League 2 season, Ljungberg eased Bukayo in gently, bringing him on as a sub for the last fifteen or twenty minutes. It didn't take long, however, for him to make a major impact for the Arsenal Under-23s.

Less than ten minutes into his debut against Manchester City, Bukayo got the ball on the left wing and burst forward, using his skill to beat the first defender and then his speed to beat the second. He was into the box now, but he didn't get carried away and waste his big opportunity. Instead, he had the composure and awareness to spot a teammate in the middle and deliver a perfect pass. Goal for Stephy Mavididi, and a first assist for Bukayo!

'Well done, mate – that was brilliant!' his teammates congratulated him.

A week later against a strong Brighton side, Bukayo did it again. The score was 0–0 with five minutes left when he got the ball and dribbled directly at the right-back, challenging him to try and stop him. Arsenal's super sub was clearly faster, so the defender tried to outmuscle him instead, but Bukayo was far too strong and determined for that. With a clever cut-back, he fooled the right-back and set up Reiss Nelson to score. 1–0 and another awesome Saka assist!

As the Arsenal players celebrated together, Bukayo got just as many high-fives and hugs as Reiss the goalscorer, if not more. He was starring for the Under-23s already and he was still sixteen years old for another two weeks.

Bukayo's seventeenth birthday turned out to be his best one yet because he got the present he had been really wishing for – his first professional football contract. As he sat down to sign the deal, he couldn't stop smiling. This was the moment he had been working so hard towards since the age of seven, and now it had arrived!

So, what was next for Bukayo? After four super-sub performances, Ljungberg decided that his young winger was ready to play from the start in the Premier League 2. Bukayo's first full game against Blackburn ended 0–0, but a week later against Liverpool, he was at his electric best.

Midway through the first half, Bukayo received the ball in his own half, turned, and attacked at top speed. Danger alert! After a one-two with Eddie Nketiah, he dribbled all the way into the Liverpool box, where he calmly curled a shot past the keeper and into the bottom corner. *1–0!*

Goooooooooooooooooooooaaaaaaaaaaaaaaaallllllllllllllll llllllllllll!!!!!!!!!!!!!!!!!!!

What a run and what a way to score his first Premier League 2 goal! Bukayo was buzzing with pride and excitement, but he didn't race off to celebrate on his own like a superstar. No, Arsenal's humble hero went straight over to high-five Eddie.

'Cheers, mate!'

After that, it was Arsenal all the way. Three minutes later, Bukayo and Tyreece pressed the Liverpool defenders until they made a mistake, passing it straight to Eddie. *2–0!*

The young Gunners looked unstoppable and especially Bukayo, who was enjoying the game of his life. Every time he got the ball, it felt like his team might score. He almost set up Tyreece for the third goal before half-time, but in the end that didn't arrive until late in the second half, when Joe Willock finished off a flowing team move. And who had played the killer final pass? Bukayo, of course!

'Thanks for the assist!' Joe cheered, throwing his arms around his awesome teammate.

'Bukayo is a great talent and played very, very well today,' his proud manager praised him after the match.

'He's just going to get better and better.'

Yes, that was the plan! That Liverpool thrashing lifted the Arsenal U-23s to the top of the Premier League 2 table. Sadly, they couldn't stay there, but Bukayo did his best to keep his team winning. Within the first ten minutes against their London rivals Chelsea, he managed to steal the ball off the right-back and then dribble through to give Arsenal the lead.

'Come onnnnn!' Bukayo yelled as he jumped up in the air and pumped his fists with passion.

But unfortunately, Chelsea fought back, just like they had in the 2018 FA Youth Cup final, winning 5–4 this time. While Bukayo was disappointed, he refused to let one defeat ruin his great start to the season. Four days later in the EFL Trophy against Forest Green Rovers, he was Arsenal's danger man yet again, creating two goals in a 3–1 victory.

The first assist in particular was a phenomenal piece of skill. From inside his own half, Bukayo dribbled the ball forward, past one defender, then another, and then another, until eventually, a fourth opponent fouled him as he entered the box. *Penalty!*

Then just two minutes after winning the spot-kick, Bukayo was back on the attack, dribbling through the Forest Green defence again. This time, he looked up and played a lovely pass through to Joe, who scored his second goal of the game.

'Yesssssssssssss!' the two young Gunners cheered together. Bukayo and Joe were on fire for the Under-23s, and Ljungberg wasn't the only Arsenal manager impressed by their performances...

CHAPTER 10

READY FOR THE FIRST TEAM PT I

'The young players are going to have chances,' Unai Emery said ahead of Arsenal's Europa League clash with Ukrainian club Vorskla Poltava, which took place on 29 November 2018. 'Some players like Eddie Nketiah, like Joe Willock, like Emile Smith Rowe, have played. Then other younger players are coming through with us like Bukayo—'

Wait a second, had the Arsenal manager really just mentioned his name at a press conference? Wow, Bukayo couldn't believe it – at the age of seventeen, his football career was moving so fast!

The Gunners had already qualified for the Last 32 with two group games to spare, so first-team stars like

Pierre-Emerick Aubameyang and Alexandre Lacazette were taking a well-earned rest. That left lots of space on the trip to Ukraine for Arsenal's most talented teenagers. After talking to Ljungberg, Emery had called up nine of the academy's best young players, including Bukayo.

'This is really happening – I'm travelling with the Arsenal first-team squad!' he reminded himself as their flight took off.

When it came to matchday, Eddie, Joe and Emile were all selected in the starting line-up, while Bukayo took his place on the bench. There, he watched and waited, praying for an opportunity to play. Even a few minutes at the end would be enough; he was just desperate to come on and make his Arsenal debut.

By half-time, Bukayo was feeling very hopeful. The Gunners were already winning 3–0, thanks to goals from Emile and Joe – surely, the manager would start making changes soon?

In the sixtieth minute, Emery took off centre-back Rob Holding and replaced him with Zech Medley.

And in the sixty-eighth minute, he took off

midfielder Aaron Ramsey and replaced him with Arsenal's new Number 87...

'Bukayo Saka!'

Twenty-five minutes – that was plenty of time for him to make a major impact in the first team. Out wide on the left wing, Bukayo controlled a long ball beautifully and then did what he did best: dribble at the defence. With a stylish stepover, he skipped away from the Vorskla right-back and opened up a very tempting route to goal. BANG! Bukayo's shot had plenty of power, but it was straight at the keeper, who made an easy save.

'Hey, cross it next time, yeah?' Eddie cried out in the middle.

'Sorry!'

The next time Bukayo got the ball in a dangerous area, he didn't cross it, but he did slip a perfectly weighted pass through to Joe, who couldn't beat the keeper either.

'Argghh noooo, great ball, Bukayo!'

He was enjoying his first-team debut so much that he really didn't want it to end, but eventually it did.

As he shook hands with the Vorskla players at the final whistle, Bukayo hoped that he had done enough to earn himself a second senior Arsenal appearance soon.

He didn't need to worry; his next opportunity actually came just two weeks later, when he was selected in Arsenal's eighteen-man squad for their last Europa League group game, at home against Qarabağ. On the day before the match, the news got even better: this time, he was going to be in the starting line-up, alongside Lacazette and Mesut Özil in attack!

Woah, was he dreaming? That night, Bukayo hardly slept at all because his brain was buzzing with football fantasies, both good and bad. What would it be like to play in front of 60,000 fans at the Emirates? What if he scored a wondergoal on his home debut? Or what if he made a bad mistake that caused his team to lose the match?

Bukayo wasn't the only member of the Saka family who struggled to sleep that night. His proud dad was feeling the same mix of nerves and excitement. On the one hand, he couldn't wait to see his son play for the Arsenal first team, a moment he had been looking forward to for years. But on the other hand, what if he had a bad game and got booed by the crowd? That could really knock his kid's confidence.

But in the biggest match of his football career so far, and with his whole family there watching, Bukayo showed no fear. Early on, he collected a pass from Mesut and curled a ferocious shot towards the top corner. The keeper saved it, but it was a clear sign that Bukayo meant business. Whether he was at Hale End or the Emirates, he was going to play the same way he always played – direct and dangerous.

'Unlucky, keep going!' Emery encouraged him from the sidelines.

Midway through the second half, Bukayo got a better chance to score. Ainsley Maitland-Niles's cutback travelled across the six-yard box until it landed at Bukayo's right foot. His quick reaction shot looked like it was heading in, but at the last second, it took a deflection off a defender and flew wide.

Ooooo, so close to his dream coming true, so close to becoming Arsenal's youngest-ever European scorer!

Sadly, Bukayo's bad luck continued. Ten minutes later, he beat the Qarabağ right-back with a beautiful bit of skill and then whipped in a cross for Eddie, who flicked the ball in with his head. *GOAL!* No, unfortunately, the linesman's flag was up. *Noooooooooooo!*

Then with seconds to go, Eddie broke away on the counterattack and slid the ball across to Bukayo, who was unmarked at the back post. He seemed certain to score, but the keeper dived down and made a super save. *NOOOOOOOO!* Why had he gone for power, instead of placing it in the corner? Oh well, never mind, Arsenal had still won the game and Bukayo had made a major impact with his courage and skill.

'He was absolutely brilliant!' said England legend Michael Owen on TV after the match.

So what if he was still only seventeen? With his excellent Europa League performances, Bukayo was pushing for a regular place in the Arsenal first team.

CHAPTER 11

READY FOR THE
FIRST TEAM PT II

Were Bukayo's years at Hale End almost over? He
continued to play most matches for the Arsenal Under-
23s, but he was training with his first team heroes at
London Colney now.

Every day, he was doing passing drills with Mesut
and Aaron,

Dribbling at Héctor Bellerín,

Creating chances for Auba and Alexandre,

And practising shots against Petr Čech.

'I still can't believe this is really happening!' Bukayo
laughed with Emile and Joe at the end of another
enjoyable session.

Arsenal's young winger wasn't getting carried away,

though. No, as his dad liked to remind him, Bukayo still had a long way to go and lots to learn. Two promising performances didn't make him a superstar, but working up close with amazing players like Auba and Mesut was definitely helping him to improve.

'Well done, Bukayo – that's a much better strike!'

Less than a month after making his Europa League debut, Bukayo found himself on the subs bench with Eddie for Arsenal's game against Burnley. In the Premier League! The excited young Gunners waited impatiently for their chance, but with the team only winning 2–1, Emery decided to bring on more experienced players instead.

A week later, Bukayo stayed on the bench against Liverpool at Anfield too, but he got third time lucky on New Year's Day. With Arsenal beating Fulham 3–1 at the Emirates, he came on for the final ten minutes, becoming the first player born in the twenty-first century to play in a Premier League match. What a proud moment it was for Bukayo and his family, and once again, he made an immediate impact.

Bukayo had only been on the pitch for a few

seconds when the ball landed at his feet on the edge
of the Fulham box. In a flash, he played it forward to
his teammate, Sokratis Papastathopoulos, who passed
it wide to Auba. His shot flicked off a defender's foot,
looped up over the keeper's head, and landed in the
net. *4–1!*

'Come onnnnnnn!' Once Auba had finished his
trademark somersault celebration, Bukayo was the
first teammate to run over and hug him. Yes, he was
starting to feel like a proper Arsenal player now.

Although that turned out to be Bukayo's one and
only Premier League appearance of the season, he
was happy with his progress, and so was his first team
manager.

'Saka is in the academy, growing up with good
performances,' Emery praised him. 'It is the beginning,
I hope, of a long career here at Arsenal.'

Yes, please – Bukayo loved the sound of that! It was
the dream he was working towards, day after day,
match after match. He was determined to make it to
the top, however long it took.

Other than a very brief sub appearance in the FA

Cup Third Round against Blackpool, Bukayo spent the second half of the 2018–19 season with Ljungberg and the Under-23s. That first taste of life in the Arsenal first team, however, had made him hungry for more. Hopefully, if he performed well in the Premier League 2, Emery would want him back there very soon…

Against Manchester City, Bukayo got the ball on the left side of the box and decided to try something a bit different. Yes, his left foot was still stronger, but he had been working hard on his right. So, to prove it, Bukayo cut inside and blasted the ball into the bottom corner with his weaker foot. *1–0!*

Gooooooooooooooooooooaaaaaaaaaaaaaaaaalllllllllllllllllllllllllll!!!!!!!!!!!!!!!!!!!!!!

'Yessssssss!' Bukayo yelled, jumping up to punch the air with both fists. In the second half, he added a second goal with his left foot to make it 4–1 to Arsenal. The movement, the first touch, the finish – his all-round play was getting better and better.

'He's learning all the time,' Ljungberg said afterwards. 'I'm very happy with him.'

And Bukayo wasn't just scoring goals of his own; he

was setting them up for his Arsenal teammates too: a lay-off to Xavier against Brighton, a cross for Tyreece against Derby, and the most important assist of all, a through-ball to Eddie in a 3–1 win over rivals Chelsea.

'Thanks, B – you're the best!' Eddie shouted to Bukayo as they celebrated the goal together. With their speed and skill, they made such a dangerous attacking duo, and they always seemed to know where to find each other on the pitch.

In their final game of the Premier League 2 season against Leicester City, Bukayo played a part in all three Arsenal goals, and all within the opening ten minutes.

First, he burst into the box and was fouled. *Penalty – 1–0!*

Then a minute later, he made a really clever run from the left wing to collect Ben Sheaf's pass, before crossing the ball to Tyreece. *2–0!*

And finally, Tyreece returned the favour by setting one up for Bukayo, who calmly slid the ball past the keeper. *3–0!*

Gooooooooooooooooooooaaaaaaaaaaaaaaaalllllllllllllll llllllllll!!!!!!!!!!!!!!!!!!!

Surely he was now too good to stay in the Under-23s? The Arsenal senior manager seemed to think so. In May, Emery named Bukayo in his matchday squad for the Europa League final against Chelsea. Although Bukayo stayed on the bench as his team lost 4–1, it was still an amazing experience that gave him extra confidence in his own ability. Yes, next season, he would be ready to play regularly for the Arsenal first team.

CHAPTER 12

A SEPTEMBER TO REMEMBER

Bukayo's big breakthrough year of 2019 got off to a great start when he was selected to go on Arsenal's preseason US tour. Some of the senior players were still on their summer holidays, and so it was a massive opportunity for the young Gunners to step up and show how good they were.

'Let's do this!' Bukayo told his old academy teammates before kick-off against the Colorado Rapids. He scored Arsenal's first goal, James Olayinka smashed home the second, and Gabriel Martinelli grabbed the third. Right, now they were ready for the main event – the International Champions Cup.

First up: German giants Bayern Munich. The match

was heading for a 1–1 draw, until in the eighty-eighth minute, when Bukayo curled a corner into the box and Tyreece set up Eddie to score the winner.

'Yesssssss!' the young Gunners celebrated together. It was a goal made at Hale End, the home of Arsenal's amazing academy.

The young stars shone brightly in the second game against Fiorentina too. On the left wing, Bukayo used his strength and skill to flick the ball on to Sead Kolašinac, who crossed it in for Eddie to score again. *1–0!*

What a terrific team move – it was football played the Arsenal way!

'The players coming up from the academy are so special,' Bukayo boldly declared in a post-match interview. 'The next generation of us can be in this Arsenal team and take on the world.'

In their final game against Real Madrid, Bukayo came off the bench and almost set up another winning goal for his friend Eddie. The cross was perfect, but the header went just wide of the post.

'Ohhhhhhhhh!' Bukayo groaned, throwing his arms

up in disappointment.

There had to be a winner, and so in the end, the match went all the way to penalties. Bukayo took Arsenal's third and coolly fired the ball into the corner of the goal, giving Thibaut Courtois no chance.

'Nice one, B!' Eddie clapped and cheered.

Another shoot-out, another successful Bukayo spot-kick, and unfortunately, another defeat for his team. Nacho Monreal and Robbie Burton both missed for Arsenal, handing the trophy to Real Madrid. Oh well, the young Gunners had done themselves proud in preseason and they all returned to London with high hopes for the months ahead.

So, what about Bukayo? He didn't get to play for the first team at all in August, but in mid-September, another chance finally arrived. For Arsenal's Europa League group game against Eintracht Frankfurt, Emery picked a very exciting new attack. Auba would be the central striker, supported by three of Hale End's finest: Emile, Joe, and Bukayo.

'Let's do this!'

From the moment the match kicked off, Bukayo

was the best player on the pitch. The Frankfurt defenders had no idea how to stop him. He almost set up a goal within the first five minutes, but Lucas Torreira's shot flew over the bar.

So close! Bukayo kept on creating brilliant chances until eventually, in the thirty-eighth minute, the goal came. After carrying the ball forward from his own half, he fed it through to Joe, who dribbled into the box and beat the keeper. 1–0 to Arsenal at last!

It stayed that way until the eighty-fifth minute, when Nicolas Pépé raced up the right wing on the counterattack. Looking up, he spotted Bukayo unmarked in the middle, just outside the box.

As the pass arrived, the Frankfurt defenders backed away, allowing Bukayo even more space for the shot. Why not? He deserved to have a go after playing so well all game. Shifting the ball to the left, he sent the ball dipping and swerving past the keeper and into the bottom corner. *2–0!*

Gooooooooooooooooooooaaaaaaaaaaaaaaaallllllllllllll llllllllllll!!!!!!!!!!!!!!!!!!!!

Yesssssss, Bukayo had scored his first senior goal for

Arsenal, and what a strike it was! He threw his arms out wide as he ran over to the fans and then blew them a big kiss.

He already had a goal and an assist, but Bukayo still wasn't done. Three minutes later, he tackled the ball off a Frankfurt defender and poked it through for Auba to score. 3–0! With a big smile on his face, the Arsenal striker turned to thank Bukayo for the assist.

'B, you're on fire!'

At the final whistle, as they walked around the pitch together arm in arm, Auba pointed at Bukayo, as if to say to the supporters, 'This guy is going to be great!'

As a reward for his breakthrough performance, Emery soon handed Bukayo his first Premier League starts: at home at the Emirates against Aston Villa, and then away at Old Trafford.

Woah, Manchester United vs Arsenal – talk about a big match! Standing on the pitch before kick-off, Bukayo's mind went back to his first trip to the stadium ten years earlier, with his dad, aged eight. So much had changed since then – now, he was there as a professional footballer, playing for his boyhood club.

Sometimes, Bukayo still couldn't believe that all this was really happening, but he was determined to make the most of every single opportunity. Each time he got the ball at Old Trafford, he looked to attack the United defence, as quickly and as skilfully as possible. In the thirtieth minute, Bukayo burst between two opponents and passed it across to Nicolas, who skied his shot high over the bar. Then just before half-time, he dribbled towards goal and forced David de Gea to make a good save.

'Unlucky – keep going, Saka!' the Arsenal supporters urged him on. Bukayo was fast becoming a real fans' favourite.

At the start of the second half, the Gunners were 1–0 down, and in need of a hero to save the day. Auba? Bukayo? Or how about both of them, working together?

In the fifty-seventh minute, the United defence gifted the ball straight to Bukayo, thirty yards out from goal. A lot of players in that position would probably have taken a touch to control it first, but Arsenal's

smart young winger was thinking ahead. He played a
first-time pass through to Auba, who chipped a shot
past de Gea. *1–1!*

Or was it? The linesman's flag was up, but after a
VAR check… the goal was given!

'Yesssssss!' Bukayo cheered as he ran over to
celebrate with his teammates. Arsenal were level and
he had his first-ever Premier League assist! The first of
many, it would soon turn out.

CHAPTER 13

LEARNING AT LEFT-BACK

Just two months after Bukayo's assist against Manchester United, Arsenal decided that it was time to change their manager. Out went Emery and in came Mikel Arteta.

Arteta had spent five successful seasons at the club as a player, before moving to Manchester City in 2016 to become Pep Guardiola's assistant. Now, after learning from the best, he was back to build a new Arsenal team capable of winning top trophies again.

'We all know there is a lot of work to be done to achieve that, but I am confident we'll do it,' Arteta announced at his first press conference. 'I'm realistic enough to know it won't happen overnight but the current squad has plenty of talent and there is a great pipeline of young players coming through from the academy.'

Phew, Bukayo was really relieved to hear his new manager mention Arsenal's youngsters. Hopefully, they would all be a big part of his ambitious plan for the future. For his first game in charge against Bournemouth, Arteta named four of them in the squad: Bukayo and Reiss in the starting eleven, plus Emile and Joe on the bench. That was great, but Bukayo wouldn't be playing on the left wing as before. No, instead he was about to become Arsenal's new left-back.

Why? Well, the main reason was that the club had a long list of injuries in defence, which included:

Centre-backs Sokratis and Rob Holding,

Right-back Héctor Bellerín,

And both main left-backs, Sead Kolašinac and Kieran Tierney.

Ainsley Maitland-Niles could also play on the left, but he was needed at right-back. So, that left only one option: Bukayo!

No problem, Bukayo was willing to do anything to help his team and to stay in the Arsenal starting line-up. It wasn't going to be easy, though. He had played at left-back before, but mostly for the England youth teams, where his main role was to attack. To do it in the Premier League, however, he was going to need to be able to defend as well. Luckily, he knew a very kind teammate who could help him with that.

'Push out – you're playing him onside!'

'That's your man – don't lose him!'

David Luiz had been giving him lots of advice and guidance ever since he first arrived at Arsenal, but now that they were going to be in defence together, Bukayo needed the Brazilian's help more than ever, in training and out on the pitch too. There was so much for him to learn: who to mark; when to wait and when to tackle; and most importantly of all, when to stay back and when to sprint forward. But with David by his side at centre-back, hopefully Bukayo could do a decent job at left-back for his team.

'I know this isn't your favourite position, but think of it as a challenge,' Arteta told him once he'd announced his first Arsenal team. 'Go out there and show me that you've got the intelligence and skill to play anywhere on the football pitch. I believe in you.'

Although Bukayo did his best against Bournemouth, it definitely wasn't his greatest game in an Arsenal shirt. In attack, his deliveries weren't as dangerous as usual, and in defence, he got caught out of position for the opening goal. When Dan Gosling tackled him, Bukayo was too high up the pitch, and as hard as he tried, he couldn't chase back in time to stop Bournemouth from scoring.

'Sorry!' he muttered miserably to his teammates as he gasped for breath.

Many young players would have struggled after making an error like that in a Premier League match, but Bukayo stayed strong. One of the things that managers loved most about him was his positive attitude. He worked hard, he never gave up, and he always learned quickly from his mistakes. So, he battled on until the final whistle, helping Arsenal to fight back for a draw. And with every game he played at left-back, his confidence grew and his defending got even better.

Against Chelsea, Bukayo tracked Tariq Lamptey's run all the way and slid in to make a good clean tackle.

'Hurray!' the Arsenal fans cheered.

Then against Sheffield United, he bravely headed away John Fleck's free kick as it curled towards the six-yard box.

'Well done, B!' David shouted next to him.

A month later, Arsenal took on Bournemouth again, this time in the FA Cup fourth round. For Bukayo, it was the perfect chance to show his manager and the supporters just how much he had improved since their last meeting. But before he could do any real defending, he was off on the attack...

In the fifth minute, Joe carried the ball forward from midfield, and then slid a pass across to Gabriel Martinelli on edge of the box. He thought about shooting himself, but instead, he played the ball through to Arsenal's new overlapping left-back: Bukayo!

As he looked up, he saw Eddie and Joe waiting in

the middle for the cross, but Bukayo had a better idea. With a fierce swing of his left leg, he blasted the ball into the top corner from a really tight angle. 1–0!

Goooooooooooooooooooaaaaaaaaaaaaaaaalllllllllllllll llllllllllll!!!!!!!!!!!!!!!!!!!!

'Yessssssss!' Bukayo cheered as he jumped up to bump chests with Gabriel. What a strike! It was his third goal for Arsenal, and his first in the FA Cup.

With his confidence up, Bukayo kept bombing forward again and again, and Bournemouth just couldn't cope with his speed and skill. In the twenty-fifth minute, Joe picked him out with a lovely pass from right to left, and Bukayo delivered a low, accurate cross to Eddie in the centre. *2–0!*

Joe to Bukayo to Eddie – it was another beautiful, flowing Arsenal team move, and the best thing about it was that it was made entirely at Hale End. As the three rising stars celebrated together in front of their excited fans, the club's future looked very bright indeed.

CHAPTER 14

ARSENAL'S MR ASSIST

Bukayo's phone was buzzing non-stop after his man-of-the-match performance against Bournemouth.

'Great game, bro!' texted Yomi Jr.

'So proud of you!' wrote his mum.

There was a nice message from his dad too, although as always Yomi Sr also had a few suggestions for ways in which his son could improve.

'Thanks, Dad. Don't worry, I know I'm not a Premier League superstar yet!'

After a challenging start, Bukayo was now enjoying life as Arsenal's new left-back. He loved his club and he loved his manager too. The guy was a genius; he knew so much about football! Arteta had a clear plan for how he wanted his team to play and he prepared them well for every game to try and outsmart their opponents. Yes, Bukayo was down as a defender on the teamsheet, but really, his role was to race up the wing and join the Arsenal attack as often as possible.

'Yes, Boss!'

In the Premier League, Bukayo caused all kinds of problems for the Newcastle United defence. As soon as Auba got the ball on the left wing, he was off on the overlap, sprinting into the space behind the right-back, Valentino Lazaro. By the time Bukayo collected the pass near the corner flag, he had two opponents in front of him, but that wasn't going to stop him. With a sudden change of speed, he skipped away from Nabil Bentaleb and then slid the ball through Lazaro's legs. *Nutmeg!*

'Hurraaaaay!' the Arsenal fans cheered. It was a fantastic bit of skill, but could Bukayo deliver a great final ball to go with it? Oh yes! He had the composure to look up, spot Nicolas in the middle, and play an accurate pass to him. *2–0!* While Nicolas led the goal celebrations, there were lots of hugs and high-fives for

Bukayo too. What an assist!

Four days later, Arsenal played away at Olympiakos in the Europa League. Bukayo had to focus on defending for most of the match, but with ten minutes to go, Auba controlled the ball high on the left wing and looked up for help.

'Coming!' Bukayo thought to himself as he zoomed forward. It was time for them to team up again.

Some left-backs would have stayed behind and called for a backwards pass, but that wasn't Bukayo's style. Instead, he burst into the penalty area, and into the gap between the Olympiakos right-back and centre-backs. It was another ingenious run from Bukayo, and when Auba's pass arrived, he knew exactly what to do next. He shifted the ball out of his feet and then curled it across the six-yard box, where Alexandre was waiting to tap in. *1–0!*

'Well done, B – what a ball!' Dani Ceballos shouted as the Arsenal players all ran over to the corner flag to celebrate together. At a crucial moment in a crucial game, their youngest star had stayed calm and delivered yet again.

And for Bukayo, the important assists kept coming.
Midway through the first half against Everton, he
escaped up the left wing and curled a beautiful,
inswinging ball into the box. There, Eddie was waiting
to link-up with his old friend Bukayo once again. He
was up against four Everton defenders, but the cross
was so good that he got there first, and flicked it past
the keeper. *1–1!*

Yessss, the Gunners were back in the game! With
one arm around Eddie, Auba the captain called out for
Bukayo to join them. 'Come on, get over here, you
hero!'

'Another game ☑ Another win 💯 Another assist 🔥,'
Bukayo posted on social media after the match. It was
still only February, and he had already hit his assists
target for the season: ten across all competitions. And
what about goals? Well, now that he was a left-back,
he wasn't getting as many chances to shoot as he
used to as a winger, so three wasn't bad at all: two in
the Europa League and one in the FA Cup. He was
still waiting for his first Premier League goal, though;
hopefully, he would be able to tick off that target

really soon…

But no, in March 2020, Bukayo's breakthrough
season came to a sudden stop due to the coronavirus
pandemic. It was a very difficult and uncertain time
for everyone. How long would the lockdown last
and when would it be safe to start mixing with other
people again? No-one really knew the answers, but
Bukayo kept working hard on his fitness at home,
while he waited for football to return. At last in late
May, Premier League teams were allowed to start
training again, and in mid-June, the season resumed.

Hurray, the big smile was back on Bukayo's face,
and in Arsenal's first game against Brighton, he looked
as brilliant as ever. In the first half, he rattled the
crossbar with a stunning right-foot shot, and then in
the second, he dribbled the ball forward and set up
Nicolas to score. Another game, another assist!

But what about that long-awaited first Premier
League goal? Well, there was good news on that
front. Kieran had returned from injury, which meant
that Bukayo didn't have to stay at left-back anymore.
Hurray, he couldn't wait to play further forward again,

where he would get more chances to score, as well as assist. He had learned a lot while playing at left-back, against the best wingers in the Premier League, and now he was ready to put that new knowledge to good use on the pitch.

Away at Wolves, Bukayo started in the Arsenal front three for the first time in ages, alongside Auba and Eddie. With half-time approaching, Kieran attempted to cross the ball to Auba, but it deflected off a defender and instead bounced towards… Bukayo! He reacted in a flash, swivelling his body so that he could sweep the ball into the corner of the net. *1–0!*

Goooooooooooooooooooooaaaaaaaaaaaaaaaaaaallllllllllllll llllllllllll!!!!!!!!!!!!!!!!!!!

Sadly, there were no fans there in the stadium to see his stunning first Premier League goal, but that wasn't going to stop Bukayo from celebrating his special moment. As he jogged over to the corner flag, he pointed at the sky and then jumped up to punch the air.

'Come onnnnnnn!' he roared with passion.

Although Arsenal finished the Premier League

season in tenth place, there was plenty for the players and fans to feel positive about. No-one had expected Arteta's grand plan to succeed straight away, but step by step, the manager was building a truly exciting young team, featuring lots of talent from the academy. Bukayo, Eddie, Joe, Reiss – the future of the club was theirs, and for their next adventure, they were off to Wembley...

CHAPTER 15

TROPHY TIME!

1 August 2020, Wembley Stadium

...Because Arsenal had made it all the way to the 2020 FA Cup final! All of their players were excited for the big day, but especially the younger ones like Bukayo. As a little boy, he had dreamed of playing in huge games at Wembley, the Home of Football, which was just five miles away from his childhood home in Ealing. And to look at him now, aged eighteen, arriving at the stadium dressed up in a smart black Arsenal team suit – unbelievable!

Bukayo tried to keep himself calm by listening to his favourite music through his headphones, but his heart was pounding in his chest as he walked through the famous corridors towards the dressing room. The beat got a hundred times faster once he changed into his training kit and then jogged out onto the pitch for the warm-up. The FA Cup final at Wembley – wow, Bukayo had really reached the big-time now! This was already one of his proudest moments as a footballer, even if he stayed on the bench and didn't get to play a single minute of the match, as had happened in the Europa League final a year earlier. Hopefully, however, that wouldn't be the case this time.

Sadly, none of the young Gunners had been included in Arteta's starting line-up for the final, but they had all played a vital role in Arsenal's FA Cup run. Bukayo had been the hero in the fourth round against Bournemouth, while in the fifth round against Portsmouth, Reiss had set up the first goal and Eddie had scored the second. For the quarter-final against Sheffield United, Arteta had picked a more experienced team, but even so, Bukayo and Joe had both still made the starting line-up.

When it came to the semi-final against Manchester

City, however, Arsenal's young stars had all found
themselves on the bench together, and that's where
Bukayo stayed for the full ninety minutes, as two
great goals from Auba took them through to the FA
Cup final. Despite his disappointment at not playing,
Bukayo hadn't just sat there sulking, though. He was
a real team player, and so at the end of the game,
he had gone out on to the pitch to congratulate the
others.

'Nice one, Auba – I knew you could do it!'

But could Arsenal now beat Chelsea in the final
and lift the FA Cup trophy for a record fourteenth
time? Bukayo was full of belief in his teammates as
they walked out of the tunnel for kick-off. Forty-
five minutes later, when the players returned to the
changing room, the game was tied at 1–1. Chelsea
had started strongly, with Christian Pulisic scoring an
early goal, but Arsenal had fought back well and guess
who had grabbed the equaliser? Yes, Auba!

At 1–1, it was all to play for in the second half of
the FA Cup final, so would Arteta choose to make
any changes? No, not yet. For now, the young

Gunners would have to keep watching and waiting impatiently, but at least they weren't sitting on the bench anymore. When the game kicked off again, the manager sent them out to get warmed up along the touchline.

'Surely, that's got to be a good sign!' Eddie told Bukayo eagerly, who was trying not to get his hopes up just yet.

But then soon after the restart, Kieran went down with what looked like a serious injury. Ooooo, what substitution was Arteta going to make? Sead was a left-back too, but bringing on Bukayo would be a way more attacking move! In the end, however, Arteta didn't have to make a decision because Kieran was fit enough to play on.

Never mind – maybe Bukayo would get a chance to come on and play further up the pitch instead, like he preferred. The longer the game stayed at 1–1, the more excited the young Gunners grew. At this rate, Arsenal were definitely going to need some super subs!

That all changed in the sixty-sixth minute, though.

Following a rampaging forward run from Héctor, the ball fell to Nicolas on the edge of the Chelsea box, and he swiftly passed it left to Auba. Danger alert!

'Come on, come on,' Bukayo muttered under his breath as he watched from the other end of the pitch. 'You can do it, Auba!'

Kurt Zouma blocked him from shooting with his stronger right foot, so instead, Arsenal's striker went with his left foot, which really wasn't much weaker anyway. With a cheeky chip over the keeper, Auba landed the ball in the back of the net. *2–1!*

'Yesssss!' Bukayo yelled, throwing his arms up in the air like every other Arsenal fan. So what if he would probably now spend the rest of the game on the bench, rather than being a super sub? A trophy for his team was the most important thing.

Eddie came on for the last ten minutes, but the other young Gunners stayed watching from the sidelines and waiting for the final whistle to blow. They were almost there now – and they just needed to stay strong for a few more minutes.

It was all over, and Arsenal had won the 2020 FA

Cup! Bukayo removed his yellow substitute's bib in a hurry and rushed over to congratulate his terrific teammates.

'Mate, what a performance!' he shouted as he gave Kieran a big hug, then David, then Auba...

Soon, Arsenal's senior stars were all dancing and singing together in a big circle. But what about the young players on the bench – were they allowed to join in too?

'Come on, get over here!' Auba called out to Bukayo and the others. They had played their part in Arsenal's success, and so they deserved to celebrate too.

After collecting his winner's medal, Bukayo sat down next to David in the front row of the team photo, ready for... trophy time! Somehow, Auba managed to drop the FA Cup as he carried it over, but he raised it high at the second attempt.

Hurrrraaaaaaaaaaaaaayyyyy!

His first professional trophy – what a feeling! It was the new greatest achievement of Bukayo's life, no doubt about it. And to share it with so many of his academy friends made it extra special. The next day, Bukayo posted a photo on social media, showing him, Eddie, Joe and Reiss, all holding the FA Cup trophy together. Above it, he wrote:

'Through the years growing up at Hale End these are the moments we were dreaming of.'

CHAPTER 16

LITTLE CHILLI, ARSENAL'S NEW NUMBER SEVEN

Wow, what a breakthrough season it had been for Bukayo – four goals, twelve assists, the Europa League Young Player of the Year award, and finally, the FA Cup trophy.

What next for Arsenal's fastest rising star? Well, ahead of the 2020–21 season, his club presented Bukayo with two great gifts:

A new four-year contract...

'London is my home. Arsenal my team,' Bukayo posted on social media with a happy picture of him signing the deal next to Arteta.

...And a new shirt number.

During his first season in the Arsenal first team,

Bukayo had worn '87' on his back, before moving on to '77'. That was better, but it was still a very high number for one of their most important players to have. So, what else could they offer him?

11? No, that already belonged to Lucas Torreira.

10? No, that was Mesut's.

Okay, well what about Number 7 then? It was a proper winger's number and with Henrikh Mkhitaryan moving to Roma, the shirt was up for grabs. Alexis, Tomáš Rosický and Robert Pires had all worn '7' for Arsenal in the past. So, how did Bukayo feel about following in the footsteps of his heroes? As usual, he was calm and composed about it.

'If a club is going to give you the number seven at such a young age, it shows how much they believe in you,' Bukayo said sensibly. 'That gives me a lot of confidence. I wouldn't say it brings pressure on me… It's so exciting, you know. It's just the stuff that you dream of. The number seven, the legends before that have worn it. It's such an honour to be given that by Arsenal.'

Oh, and there was one other gift that Bukayo had

received over the summer: **a new nickname**. It all
started one day in training when Arsenal's forwards
were practising shots together. Bukayo was on fire,
striking the ball so fiercely. While he was scoring goal
after goal, Auba kept on shouting the same thing in
French, but what was it and what did it mean?

'I was calling you "*petit piment*",' Auba explained
to him afterwards. 'It means "Little Chilli" in English.
I think it suits your football style – all that power and
energy!'

After that, 'Little Chilli' stuck and all the Arsenal
players started calling him that. Bukayo loved his
awesome new nickname, especially as it had come
from the team captain himself. Auba even bought him a
special chilli necklace after they won the FA Cup.

Little Chilli's new chapter as a Number 7 kicked off
in the FA Community Shield against Premier League
champions Liverpool. It was another big game at
Wembley for Arsenal and another chance to win a
trophy. This time, however, Arteta trusted Bukayo to
start on the right side of the front three, and it didn't
take long for the plan to work.

In the eleventh minute, Héctor played a great pass down the line to Bukayo, who carried the ball forward over the halfway line. Once Virgil van Dijk stood tall in front of him, he cut inside on his left foot and delivered a diagonal ball to Auba.

It was a move that they'd been working on in training for months, and Bukayo got his long pass inch-perfect. After a quick touch to control, Auba was able to cut inside on his right foot and fire a swerving shot into the far corner. *1–0!*

With a smile and a point, the striker looked over at Little Chilli and let out a loud, 'Whoooooooooooooop!' When they linked up together like that, Arsenal's attack was unstoppable.

Six minutes later, their new Number 7 almost had his second assist of the match. Bukayo's cross to Eddie was as excellent as ever, but unfortunately he couldn't quite find a way past Alisson.

'Unlucky!' Bukayo called out encouragingly to his friend.

He was having one of those games where everything he did looked dangerous. Being super-speedy certainly helped, but Bukayo also had so much intelligence and composure for such a young player. Sometimes on the pitch, he looked like he had all the time in the world to pick out the right pass. And confidence – he had plenty of that too. At the end of the first half, Bukayo curled in a clever free kick that almost reached David in the six-yard box.

In the second half, Bukayo continued to shine, but it was Liverpool and not Arsenal who scored the second goal of the game. Mo Salah weaved his way into the box and Takumi Minamino swept the ball past Emiliano Martínez. *1–1!*

After eighty-two brilliant minutes, Bukayo's Community Shield came to an end, as Joe ran on to replace him. With fresh legs in attack, could Arsenal score a late winner? No, and neither could Liverpool, so the match went to penalties.

'Good luck – go win this!' Bukayo told his teammates as they stood together in a huddle. He really wished he was taking one himself, rather than watching on helplessly from the sidelines.

In the end, however, it turned out to be a very

successful shoot-out for the Gunners. Reiss, Ainsley, Cédric Soares and David all scored from the spot – four out of four! Then, when Rhian Brewster hit the bar for Liverpool, Auba had the chance to be the hero. He coolly stepped up and sent the keeper the wrong way. Arsenal were the winners!

With a big smile on his face, Bukayo sprinted across the pitch to join in the celebrations. First the FA Cup and now the Community Shield – his team had lifted two trophies in less than a month!

Hurrrraaaaaaaaaaaaaayyyyy!

As the Arsenal players danced around under the gold confetti at Wembley, it was all set to be a very exciting season for the club. Arteta's next challenge was to lead his young team up the Premier League table and back into the Top Four.

Arsenal won their first two games against Fulham and West Ham United, but at home against Sheffield United, they were really struggling to break through and score. A long-range shot from Auba flew just over the bar and Eddie's glancing header bounced up straight in front of the keeper. Sadly, that was the best of the first-half action.

What the Gunners needed in the second half was a gamechanger, and it was their new Number 7 who stepped forward to save the day. In the sixtieth minute, Auba played a pass through to Héctor, who chipped a cross over to Bukayo at the back post. Heading wasn't his best attribute, but he kept his eye on the ball and powered it into the top corner. *1–0!*

Goooooooooooooooooooaaaaaaaaaaaaaaaalllllllllllllll lllllllll!!!!!!!!!!!!!!!!!!!!

Yessssss, Little Chilli!

Bukayo to the rescue! Even though there were no supporters there to see his first goal at the Emirates, he still slid towards the corner flag on his knees. He was a proper Premier League star now, and he was about to become a senior England star too.

CHAPTER 17

RISING THROUGH THE ENGLAND RANKS

Ever since the Under-17 Euros in 2017, Bukayo had been working his way up steadily through the England youth teams. First, he had joined the Under-18s, where he scored a penalty to beat France and set up a goal against Sweden. Then after five matches, he moved up to the Under-19s, where he made an immediate impact. Bukayo only came on as a late substitute against Moldova, but just three minutes into his debut, he already had his first goal. There was simply no stopping him. By his fourth appearance, against the Czech Republic, he was into the starting line-up and stealing the show for England.

Early in the first half, Bukayo raced onto Angel

Gomes's through-ball, shrugged off his marker, and coolly fired a shot past the keeper. *GOAL!*

'Let's go!' Grabbing the ball from the net, he ran straight back for the restart, high-fiving his teammates along the way.

Early in the second half, Bukayo created a chance for Marc Guéhi to score. *ASSIST!*

Then seven minutes later, he collected the ball on the left wing and beat the keeper again with a powerful low strike. *GOAL!*

Wow, what an impressive performance, and the best part for Bukayo was that Southgate had been there watching at St George's Park. Suddenly, he was on a fast track to the top. After just one game for the Under-21s, in September 2020, Bukayo received some very exciting news in October.

The Arsenal team were landing in Liverpool to play a Premier League match, and Bukayo switched his phone off airplane mode to find a message from a name and number that he didn't recognise. The first line, however, made his heart beat a lot faster:

'Congratulations Bukayo, you've been called up to

the England senior team.'

What?! He didn't even read the rest of the message. Instead, Bukayo just sat there in shock, staring at his phone screen, until eventually, Alexandre came over and hit him in the head.

'Come on, we have to get off the plane!'

Bukayo really couldn't believe it; at the age of nineteen, he was about to become a senior international already! 'Honoured and grateful to get my first England call up,' he tweeted with a photo of him proudly wearing the three lions on his shirt.

It was a dream come true to be training alongside heroes like Harry Kane, Jordan Henderson, Kyle Walker and Raheem Sterling, but Bukayo didn't let that faze him. He had earned his place in the squad through years of hard work, and this was his chance to show everyone that he was ready to star for his country. There was no way he was going to waste it.

The games against Belgium and Denmark were both proper UEFA Nations League matches, but first, England were taking on Wales in a friendly. It was a great opportunity for Southgate to test out some of his less experienced players, like Dominic Calvert-Lewin, Kalvin Phillips, Jack Grealish… and Bukayo!

Brilliant news – he was going to make his England senior debut, but what position would his manager ask him to play?

Left wing? No, not this time.

Left-back? No, not there either.

Left wing-back! No problem, Bukayo was just grateful to be picked and he was prepared to give his all for his country, wherever he played on the pitch.

After a slightly shaky start, Bukayo got better and better as the game went on. He did his defensive work when he needed to and raced forward on the attack as often as he could.

'Yes!' Bukayo called out, sprinting up the left wing and into the box. He was completely unmarked as Mason Mount slid the ball across to him – what an opportunity to get a first goal for England straight away… *BANG!* Bukayo's low shot was heading towards the bottom corner, until it deflected off the leg of a diving Welsh defender and looped up at a good height for the keeper to make the save.

Ooooooh, nearly a dream debut! Oh well, while he hadn't scored or set up any of three England goals, Bukayo was still proud to have played his first game for the senior team.

'A massive achievement for me last night making my full England debut!' he posted on social media. 'What an absolute privilege. I would like to thank everyone for the support and messages. The journey continues...'

Bukayo didn't get to play in the games against Belgium or Denmark, but a month later, he was back in the starting line-up for another friendly, against the Republic of Ireland. Second time around, Bukayo really took his chance to shine. He was involved in almost everything for England.

Early on, he raced forward and delivered a teasing cross into the box, which an Irish defender headed behind. *Unlucky!*

Ten minutes later, he snuck in at the back post, but the keeper managed to block his shot just in time. *So close!*

Just before half-time, he was almost through on

goal again, but a defender intercepted the pass at the last second. *Nearly!*

Early in the second half, Tyrone Mings set Bukayo up with a beautiful backheel, but his poked shot hit the side-netting instead. *Noooo!*

With a hand over his mouth, he looked to the sky in shock. Bukayo was playing so well, but why couldn't he finish off any of these amazing chances?

When Dominic then headed the ball wide from his incredible cross, Bukayo really thought it was just going to be one of those frustrating days where nothing quite worked out. A few minutes later, however, he finally got the reward he deserved.

Collecting the ball wide on the left wing, Bukayo dribbled infield towards the Ireland right-back, Cyrus Christie, tempting him to try and tackle him. With a stepover and a burst of speed, he escaped past the defender, who clipped his right leg as he entered the box. Penalty!

Dominic scored from the spot and then went straight over to celebrate with the player who had created the goal with his skilful run.

'Nice one, B!' the striker shouted as they high-fived together.

After the final whistle, Bukayo was awarded the Man of the Match trophy for his dangerous attacking display and he received praise from his England manager too.

'Bukayo on the left looked a lot more confident than in his first game,' Southgate said.

As ever, his timing was excellent because the Euros were now just seven months away.

CHAPTER 18

ARSENAL'S MR ANYWHERE

Back at Arsenal, Bukayo continued to perform well in lots of different positions. One game he was in central midfield against Manchester City, the next he was on the left wing against Leicester City, and the next he was at left-back against Manchester United. He was Arsenal's Mr Anywhere!

It was great to be so versatile, but what was Bukayo's best position of all? For a while, Arteta thought that it was left wing, but when his team went on a losing run, he decided to try switching his player over to the right instead. It turned out to be one of his best decisions as Arsenal manager.

It all started in the London derby against Chelsea,

where Arteta picked Alexandre as the central striker, supported by three of Hale End's finest: Gabriel, Bukayo and Emile. How exciting! Bukayo was delighted to see his good friend Emile back after loan spells at RB Leipzig and Huddersfield Town. Together, Arsenal's next generation were ready to take on the world.

Early in the second half, Emile passed the ball to Bukayo as he burst into the right side of the box. With his first touch, he dribbled further into the penalty area, but the Chelsea defenders still didn't try to close him down. 'He can't use his left foot there, so he probably won't shoot,' they must have thought, but with his second touch, Bukayo sent the ball flying towards goal with a whip of his 'weaker' right foot. Was it a cross or was it a shot? No-one really knew, but his powerful strike sailed over Édouard Mendy's head, hit the post, and went in.

Goooooooooooooooooooooaaaaaaaaaaaaaaaalllllllllllllll llllllllllll!!!!!!!!!!!!!!!!!!!!

'Yesssss, B – what a shot!' Emile cheered, giving his friend a hug. 'That was a shot, right?'

'Of course!' Bukayo replied with a big grin on his face. Besides, who cared if he meant to do it or not? He had scored, his team were winning, and surely that was all that mattered.

That wondergoal against Chelsea was the beginning of Bukayo's best-ever run of form, as he won the Arsenal Player of the Month awards for December, January and February.

Against Brighton, he dribbled forward from his own half and set up Alexandre to score the winner. *ASSIST!*

Then a few days later, playing in the snow against West Brom, he scored one of Arsenal's best goals of the season. The move began with Emile, who played a first-time pass through to Bukayo, who spun and gave the ball to Alexandre. Alexandre played a first-time pass through to Emile, who had continued his run into the box, and he slid the ball across to Bukayo, who couldn't miss.

Gooooooooooooooooooooaaaaaaaaaaaaaaaaalllllllllllllll llllllllllll!!!!!!!!!!!!!!!!!!!!

Wow, what a brilliant, flowing team move! A

beaming Bukayo pointed over at Emile and then waved his arms up and down wildly. It was so much fun playing football with his friends.

The next week against Newcastle United, Arsenal's young stars teamed up again. Emile dribbled in off the left wing and picked out Bukayo near the penalty spot. With a sweep of his left foot, he fired the ball past the keeper first-time.

Goooooooooooooooooooooaaaaaaaaaaaaaaaaaallllllllllllll llllllllllll!!!!!!!!!!!!!!!!!!!

'Mate, you're the best!' he cheered, pointing over at Emile once more.

Now that Bukayo was on the right wing, Arsenal were winning games and rising up the Premier League table. Away at Southampton, they went 1–0 down, but young Bukayo led the fightback. First, he dribbled around the keeper and scored, and then he set up Alexandre to secure another victory.

'Goal, assist and 3 points,' he tweeted afterwards. 'A perfect Tuesday night.'

In the space of just one season, Bukayo had gone from a star for the future to become one of Arsenal's most important players. Now, when he wasn't in the team, they usually lost, but when he was fit and firing, they usually won. Against Leeds United, Bukayo played a one-two with Emile and then just kept running forward with the ball until finally a defender fouled him in the box. *Penalty!*

Or was it? No, in the end, VAR overruled the referee's decision, but six minutes later, Bukayo rushed in to steal the ball off the Leeds keeper and was fouled again. This time, the penalty was given, and Auba scored from the spot. *2–0!*

But Bukayo wanted more and there was nothing that Leeds could do to stop him. Before half-time, he led Arsenal on another attack, which ended in a goal for Héctor. 3–0! Then early in the second half, he charged forward again. Eventually, the ball came to Emile, who set up Auba to complete his first-ever Premier League hat-trick. *4–0!*

It was now obvious that right wing was Bukayo's best position, but when his team needed him to adapt, he was still happy to be Arsenal's Mr Anywhere. He played in central midfield against Sheffield United, on the left wing against Aston Villa, and then, when against West Brom, he moved back to left-back, where he made lots of his old overlapping runs.

Racing onto a pass from Willian, Bukayo looked up and delivered a dangerous ball into the six-yard box. It was an excellent cross, but could any of his teammates get on the end of it? Oh yes, Emile knew what to expect from his friend and he arrived at exactly the right moment to volley it in.

'Thanks, B!' he called out as they high-fived and hugged. Together, they were living their childhood Premier League dream.

That win lifted Arsenal into the top-half of the table again at last, but they finished in ninth position, outside of the European places. Sadly, it hadn't been the successful season that the fans had hoped for, but at least their young stars Bukayo and Emile had been shining lights, both in the Premier League and in the Europa League.

CHAPTER 19

ELECTRIC IN THE EUROPA LEAGUE AGAIN

Bukayo loved all football competitions, but the Europa League would always be extra special for him. After all, it was where he had made his Arsenal first team debut back in 2018, plus where he had grabbed his first senior goal and assist. During the 2019–20 season, he had played so well that he won the Europa League Young Player of the Year award, so what next for 2020–21?

Well, during the group stage, Bukayo hardly played at all, but it wasn't because he wasn't good enough to make the starting line-up. No, it was because Arteta wanted to give him a well-earned rest. But once Arsenal reached the knockout rounds, Bukayo was straight back in the team and straight back on the scoresheet.

Against Benfica, the Gunners went 1–0 down, but they didn't stay behind for long. Less than two minutes later, Cedric fired a long cross into the crowded penalty area, and there was Bukayo, waiting to coolly sweep the ball in like an experienced striker. *1–1!*

Goooooooooooooooooooooaaaaaaaaaaaaaaaaallllllllllllllll lllllllllllll!!!!!!!!!!!!!!!!!!!!

Thanks to Bukayo, Arsenal returned home with a vital away goal, but in the second leg back at the Emirates, he still had more game-changing work to do.

In the twentieth minute, Bukayo dribbled in off the right wing and split the Benfica defence with a brilliant angled pass through to Auba. *2–1!*

'Thanks, Little Chilli!' his captain called out as they shared a high-five together.

At that point, it looked like Arsenal were heading safely through to the Europa League Last 16, but forty disastrous minutes later, they found themselves 3–2 down and on their way out of the competition. Unless their heroes could save the day…

Kieran scored the equaliser to make it 3–3, and with five minutes to go, Arsenal were on the attack again, searching for a winning goal. When the ball arrived at Bukayo's feet, he was out wide on the right wing, but he dribbled his way into the box at speed. What now? There was still a defender blocking his path, so he used a double stepover to create a bit of space for himself. Then with his left foot, Bukayo curled a beautiful cross towards the back post, and Auba raced in to meet it with his head. *4–3 to Arsenal!*

In the next round, the Gunners cruised past Olympiakos without too much drama, to set up a quarter-final clash with Slavia Prague. The Czech club had already beaten Leicester City and Rangers in the competition, and now they were aiming to complete a British hat-trick.

In the first leg at the Emirates, Arsenal dominated the game, but they missed chance after chance after chance. Bukayo shot wide, Rob Holding's header was tipped over, Willian's free kick clipped the post, and then Alexandre's strike crashed against the crossbar. Nooooo, why oh why wouldn't the ball go in the net?

Finally, in the eighty-sixth minute, a goal arrived for Arsenal. Auba poked a pass through to Nicolas and he lifted the ball over the diving keeper. *1–0!* At last, they were winning, but deep in injury time, all their hard work was undone. They failed to defend a corner-kick and Tomáš Holeš snuck in at the back post to equalise for Slavia Prague, and give them a huge away goal.

It was a really frustrating result for Arsenal, but at least they had the second leg to put things right. Away in Prague at the Sinobo Stadium, the Gunners bounced back with a stunning performance, and Bukayo was the best player on the pitch. The poor Slavia left-back, Jan Bořil, didn't stand a chance against him.

In the thirteenth minute, Bukayo left Bořil trailing behind as he cut inside and unleashed a powerful shot that bounced off the post and fell straight to Emile for an easy tap-in. *1–0!* But no, after a VAR check, the goal was disallowed for offside. Oh well, they would just have to keep attacking...

Five minutes later, Emile used some fancy footwork to set up Nicolas, and this time the goal counted. *1–0!*

Hurray, they had an away goal already, and the young Gunners were hungry for more. As Emile raced up the right wing with the ball, Bukayo burst into the box, ready for the cross. But when it arrived, a Slavia player bundled straight into the back of him. Penalty! Alexandre stepped up to score from the spot. *2–0!*

When they passed and moved like that, Arsenal's young forwards just had far too much speed and skill for the Czech defenders. From the right wing, Bukayo skipped inside past Bořil with ease and then fired an unstoppable shot into the bottom corner. *3–0!*

Goooooooooooooooooooaaaaaaaaaaaaaaaaallllllllllllll llllllllllll!!!!!!!!!!!!!!!!!!!

And game over. The Slavia manager decided to take Bořil off at half-time, while Bukayo played on until the eightieth minute, when Arteta finally gave him a well-earned rest after another electric night in the Europa League.

'It shows everyone how exciting we can be,' Bukayo said with a big smile in his post-match interview. 'When we play like this, it is so amazing to be involved in.'

Later on social media, he posted a photo of his happy goal celebration, with a caption saying, 'Sliding into the semi-finals...'

Next up for Arsenal: Spanish club Villarreal, who were managed by... Unai Emery! Bukayo was looking forward to meeting up with his old boss again, but his focus was really on winning and helping his club to reach the Europa League final again.

'Come on, we can do this!' Bukayo told his teammates in the dressing room before the away leg in Spain. Although he was still very humble, he was no longer the quiet, shy kid who had first arrived in the Arsenal first team back in 2018. Now, he was one of their most important players, and that meant he had a responsibility to speak up and be a leader.

Before Bukayo could really have an impact on the big game, however, Villarreal raced into a two-goal lead. Then early in the second half, things got even worse for Arsenal, when Dani Ceballos was sent off. Uh-oh, it was turning into a disaster – if they weren't careful, it could all be over by the end of the first leg.

But in the last thirty minutes, Arsenal fought back. Their defenders stood strong, and their attackers went in search of an away goal. From wide on the right wing, Bukayo passed to Emile and then moved infield for the return pass. When the ball came back to him, he was just outside the box, so Bukayo dribbled bravely on forward, daring a Villarreal defender to try and tackle him. Manu Trigueros couldn't resist the challenge, but he failed to get the ball, kicking Bukayo's leg instead. *Penalty!*

'Well done, B!' Emile exclaimed as he helped his friend back up to his feet.

Nicolas scored the spot-kick to keep Arsenal's Europa League dream alive, but they still had goals to get in the second leg at the Emirates. So, where were they going to come from?

Auba? No, he hit the post twice, first with a volley and then with a header.

Nicolas? No, his swerving shot flew wide.

Emile? No, his chip missed the target too.

Bukayo? No, sadly he was having a really

disappointing night. As hard as he tried, he just couldn't find a way past the Villarreal left-back, and when he switched wings to the left, he struggled against their right-back too.

'Arghhhh!' he cried out, kicking the air in frustration.

At the final whistle, the score was still 0–0, which meant Arsenal were out of the Europa League. There would be no trip to the final, and that wasn't all; after finishing ninth in the Premier League, they wouldn't be playing in the competition next season either.

As the bad news sunk in, Bukayo walked slowly around the pitch for ages, shaking his head and staring down at the grass. He felt like he had really let the Arsenal fans down. It was one of the worst moments of his football career so far, but fortunately, more exciting times were just around the corner.

CHAPTER 20

EURO 2020: ENGLAND'S SURPRISE STAR

Yes, soon after that miserable night in May 2021, Bukayo would enjoy one of the best weeks of his life. It started on Tuesday 1 June, when Southgate announced his final twenty-six-man England squad for the delayed Euro 2020, and there he was, amongst the eight forwards on the list:

'...Harry Kane (Tottenham Hotspur), Marcus Rashford (Manchester United), Bukayo Saka (Arsenal)...'

He was in, he was going to be at Euro 2020 with England! It had always been his aim to represent his country at major international tournaments, but to be doing that already, at the age of nineteen? It was beyond Bukayo's wildest dreams. 'A special summer awaits,' he tweeted with a photo of him proudly wearing the new national kit.

That was definitely enough exciting news for one day, but no, there was more; Bukayo was also on the shortlist for the Premier League Young Player of the Season award, alongside five of his England teammates: Marcus, Mason Mount, Declan Rice, Dominic Calvert-Lewin, and Phil Foden. Wow, what an honour!

The next day, Bukayo's amazing week continued when he played the full ninety minutes of England's pre-tournament match against Austria. Every match he played was a chance to impress his manager, and Bukayo was determined to make the most of what would probably be his last opportunity before Euro 2020.

It was an international friendly at the end of a long, hard season, but Bukayo looked as fit, fresh and focused as ever on the left wing for England. His passes were accurate, his runs were dangerous, and he never seemed to lose the ball, no matter how many opponents surrounded him.

In the twentieth minute, Bukayo raced in at the back post and was unlucky not to score with a volley that swerved just wide of the post. Next, he pounced on an Austrian mistake and played the ball inside to Jack, who set up a great scoring chance for Harry. Saved!

'Unlucky, well played!' Southgate cheered from the sidelines.

Early in the second half, England finally got their goal. Jack started the move on the halfway line with a forward pass to Harry on the left, who turned and slid the ball right to Jesse Lingard. Jesse tapped it through for Jack on the run, but he couldn't quite reach it before the defender. When the ball rolled loose, it looked like it might go out for a corner, but no – there was Bukayo sprinting towards it and he managed to sweep it into the net from a very tight angle. *1–0!*

Goooooooooooooooooooooaaaaaaaaaaaaaaaallllllllllllll lllllllllll!!!!!!!!!!!!!!!!!!!

After proudly tapping the Three Lions on his shirt, Bukayo punched the air with both fists. It was a moment that he had dreamed about so many times as a kid, and now he had actually done it. He had his first senior goal for England, and what a time to score it! Forty minutes later when he walked off the pitch, he was the matchwinner. Job done; Bukayo had certainly impressed his manager.

'He's like a slippery eel getting away from those challenges!' Southgate said afterwards. 'And he works well defensively for the team, so I'm really pleased with him, and for him, to get the goal.'

Thanks, Boss! And Bukayo's amazing week still wasn't over. On the Friday, he won the Arsenal Player of the Season award for his seven goals, ten assists and forty-six stellar performances.

'This is a really special moment for me in my career,' he told the fans in a video message from the England training camp. 'It's just such an honour to put the shirt on and represent you guys and feel your love and support across the season, through the good and bad times, so thank you for that.'

After that, Bukayo switched his focus back to England, where the manager now had an even bigger headache to deal with ahead of their first game of the Euros. There was still one place up for grabs in Southgate's first-choice front-three: Harry, Raheem, and who???

Would it be Marcus, or Jack, or Phil, or Jadon... or Bukayo? They all had different qualities to offer, and Bukayo's all-round display against Austria had made the decision even harder. In the end, for their opening game against Croatia, Southgate decided to go with... Phil.

Oh well, it was the bench for Bukayo and the other forwards, but they fully respected their manager's decision. Although they were all competing for a starting spot, they never felt like rivals. No, they were all working together as part of the same England team to try and win the Euros, and so the team spirit was stronger than ever.

At St George's Park, Bukayo spent a lot of time hanging out with Phil, Jadon and Jude Bellingham, the other youngest players in the squad, but he got on really well with everyone: Jack, Reece, Kalvin, Tyrone, and especially the left-back Luke Shaw. 'I would love him to be my brother,' Luke even said in an interview. 'He's so cool, he's so funny.'

While Bukayo was pleased to be a popular figure in the England squad, his aim was to play some football at the Euros. However, when he didn't come on against Croatia and he wasn't even in the squad against Scotland, he began to wonder if that would happen. Bukayo didn't give up hope, though; he carried on watching, waiting and learning as much as possible from the senior players every day in training.

After a win and a draw in their first two games, England were almost through to the Round of 16. So for their final group match against the Czech Republic, Southgate decided to make a few changes in attack. Jack replaced Mason in the central attacking midfield role, while on the right wing, Phil was rested and in came... Bukayo! It was a surprise for many England supporters who were expecting Marcus or Jadon, but they were soon cheering for their new national hero.

At last, Bukayo had his chance to play at Euro 2020, and he was determined to make the most of it, doing exactly what his manager had told him to do:

'Play with confidence and freedom.'

Yes, Boss! In the eleventh minute, Bukayo dropped deep to get the ball, and then spun and dribbled forward at speed just like he did for Arsenal. After crossing the halfway line, he passed to Kalvin, and then kept running into the box for the one-two. When the return pass arrived, Bukayo delivered a deep cross to the back post, but it was a bit too high for Harry. Never mind, Jack curled in another cross from the left side. As the ball floated across the six-yard box, Bukayo raced into the middle and leapt up high to meet it, but unfortunately, it flew just over his head. There was no need to worry, though; Raheem was right behind him and he nodded the ball into the net. *1–0!*

'Come on!' Bukayo cried out, punching the air with passion. England were winning at Wembley and he had played an important part in setting it up!

That goal was just the beginning of a brilliant individual performance. In their first two games at Euro 2020, England had looked a bit boring and slow in attack, but every time Bukayo got the ball, his first thought was to dribble forward with speed and skill. Again and again, he terrorised the Czech left-back Boril, just like he had for Arsenal against Slavia Prague. Although he couldn't quite create a second goal for his team, Bukayo was England's danger man throughout. At the final whistle, there was no doubt who the man of the match was.

'The way Saka played today,' argued Micah Richards on TV, 'he can't be dropped. He was absolutely outstanding.'

And Southgate agreed. 'He was fabulous,' the England manager said, and so for the big Round of 16 clash with Germany, Bukayo was back in the starting line-up.

Wow, it was a massive match for such a young player, but the pressure didn't bother Bukayo at all. In the tight, tense first half, he was England's stand-out star again, causing lots of problems for the German defence with his rampaging runs up the right wing.

After his strong start, Bukayo faded a bit in the second half, and in the sixty-eighth minute, Jack came on to replace him. What a smart substitution it turned out to be – Jack soon helped set up England's first goal for Raheem and then the second for Harry. At 2–0, they were going through to the quarter-finals!

When the final whistle blew, Bukayo hugged Southgate on the touchline and then headed back out onto the pitch to celebrate with his teammates in front of the 40,000 England fans. It was the first time they had beaten Germany in a knockout match at a major tournament since the 1966 World Cup.

'Special to be a part of this team,' Bukayo tweeted to his fans. 'Let's keep making history!'

Bukayo wasn't just Mr Popular amongst his teammates anymore; he was also Mr Popular across the whole entire country. The fans loved him, and when England posted photos of him jumping into the pool at St George's Park on an inflatable unicorn, they went viral straight away!

England's next opponents in the Euro quarter-finals were Ukraine. Would Bukayo be in Southgate's starting line-up again? No, he had to miss the match with a dead leg, but there was no need to worry because the team won 4–0 without him.

Bukayo was ready to return for the semi-final against Denmark and he had an important part to play again as England fought back from 1–0 down.

Just before half-time, Harry dropped deep to receive the ball, and that's when Bukayo made his move, racing from the right wing into the space behind the Denmark defence. Harry's pass was perfect, and so was Bukayo's cross into the six-yard box, where he knew Raheem would be waiting. The final touch came off a sliding defender, but who cared? England were level!

'Yesssss, B!' Raheem roared as he ran over to high-five his talented young teammate. What a tournament he was having!

On his comeback from injury, Bukayo could only last seventy minutes, but he received a standing ovation from the supporters as he left the pitch. Jack was the player who replaced him – could he be England's super sub again? No, the match went to extra-time, and in the 103rd minute, Raheem dribbled his way into the box, past one Denmark defender, and as he glided past another, he was barged in the side.

Penalty!

Now, it was up to Harry to fire England into the Euro 2020 final. His spot-kick was saved, but fortunately he reacted quickly to score the rebound. *2–1!*

Wembley went wild, and Bukayo threw his arms up in the air and let out a loud cheer on the bench. That was the best he could do because he was in too much pain to make it over to the corner flag to join the celebrations. But when at last the final whistle blew, Bukayo hobbled back onto the pitch to hug each and every one of his teammates, and then join the England players and fans in a special singalong:

Sweet Caroline,
Da-da-da,
Good times never seemed so good,
So good, so good, so good!

What a night, what an atmosphere, and what an achievement! For the first time since 1966, England were through to the final of a major tournament.

Could they now go all the way and win it?

CHAPTER 21

THE PAIN OF A PENALTY MISS

11 July 2021, Wembley Stadium

Euro 2020 final – England vs Italy

England were now just one game away from becoming European Champions for the first time ever, but Bukayo and his teammates knew that beating Italy was going to be their toughest challenge yet. The *Azzurri* had been brilliant all tournament, knocking out Belgium and Spain on their way to the final.

England, however, did have the home advantage. They were playing at Wembley, in front of over 50,000 of their fans. So, as the two teams walked out past the

Euro 2020 trophy and onto the pitch, it was 'England! England!' that the players could hear most clearly.

Unfortunately for Bukayo, however, he wasn't one of those players. For the final, Southgate had gone for a more defensive formation, with Kieran Trippier replacing him as a right wing-back. Bukayo was disappointed, of course, but he understood and respected his manager's decision. Hopefully, he would get to come on and make an impact later on in the game.

When England scored after two minutes, however, that looked less likely. From defence, Luke sent the ball forward to Harry Kane, who turned and dribbled up to the halfway line, before passing it on to Kieran, who was sprinting up the right wing. His cross sailed over Harry's head but landed perfectly for Luke, who had continued his run all the way to the back post. *1–0!*

Wow, what a start for England, but the Euro 2020 final was far from over. As the game went on, Italy grew stronger and stronger. First, Federico Chiesa fired a shot just wide of the post, and then early in the second half, he forced Jordan Pickford to stretch down and make a super save.

Phew! On the bench, Bukayo could hardly bear to watch. Come on, England! In the sixty-sixth minute, however, Italy finally got their equaliser. Bryan Cristante flicked on the corner at the front post and the ball bounced all the way through to Marco Verratti at the back post. His header hit the post, but Leonardo Bonucci was there to smash the rebound past Harry on the goal line. *1–1!*

Right, it was time for some England substitutions. Off came Kieran and on came… Bukayo! Could he use his speed and skill to create another moment of magic, like he had against the Czech Republic and Denmark? He spent most of the last twenty minutes defending deep in his own half, but just before the final whistle blew, he raced forward to press Giorgio Chiellini. The Italian centre-back tried to let the ball run out of play, but Bukayo was fast enough to run around the outside of him and get to it first. At last, this was his chance to attack! As he tried to escape towards goal, however, Chiellini stopped him by yanking hard on the back of his shirt.

Heyyyyyy!

It was a clear and obvious foul, but what colour card would the referee give him? Despite the protests of the England players, the answer was only a yellow. Never mind, Bukayo picked himself up and carried on playing. Hopefully, he would get another chance to attack in extra-time…

But no, after thirty more minutes of football, the two teams still couldn't be separated, and so the Euro 2020 final went to PENALTIES! Uh-oh, England's record in major tournament shoot-outs was terrible.

The 1990 World Cup against Germany,

Euro 1996 against Germany,

The 1998 World Cup against Argentina,

Euro 2004 against Portugal,

The 2006 World Cup against Portugal,

And Euro 2012 against Italy.

Six scary shoot-outs and the Three Lions had lost every single one!

England's penalty-taking skills had come a long way since then, though. Southgate had made sure that his players practised spot-kicks regularly in training and were well prepared for the high-pressure situation. At

the 2018 World Cup, they had successfully ended that
embarrassing run by beating Colombia, and so as they
huddled together on the Wembley pitch at the end of
the Euro 2020 final, the England team were feeling calm
and confident. They knew what they needed to do, and
Southgate knew who his five best takers were:

1) Harry Kane… placed his penalty in the bottom
corner where the Italian keeper, Gianluigi Donnarumma,
couldn't reach it. *GOAL!*

2) Harry Maguire… blasted an unstoppable shot into
the top corner. *GOAL!*

After four spot-kicks, England were winning 2–1
because Jordan had made a brilliant save to stop Andrea
Belotti's strike. The excitement was building around
Wembley Stadium – were they about to win their first
major trophy for fifty-five years? Was football finally
coming home? So far, everything was going according to
plan, but…

3) Marcus Rashford… clipped the outside of the post.
MISS!

4) Jadon Sancho… aimed for the bottom corner, but
Donnarumma dived the right way. *SAVED!*

Oh dear, now it was all down to:

5) Bukayo!

Yes, at the age of just nineteen, Southgate was trusting him to take England's last penalty, the most high-pressure of all. Was he ready for so much responsibility? Yes, Bukayo's record in training was remarkable and he had scored for the England Under-17s and for Arsenal in preseason, but this was the Euro 2020 final now!

Any doubts could wait, though, because if Italy's next spot-kick went in, the shoot-out would be over before Bukayo even stepped forward. The England fans feared the worst as Jorginho walked forward because he hardly ever missed, but Jordan guessed the right way and made the save. Hurray, England's hopes were still alive, but only if they scored their final penalty…

Bukayo made the long walk forward from the halfway line, placed the ball down on the spot, and then focused his eyes on the target in front of him. Donnarumma was so big that he seemed to fill the whole goal, but Bukayo could beat him. He could do this. After a deep breath, he got his legs pumping and then began his short run-up. He aimed for the same bottom corner as Jadon, and

again, the Italian keeper guessed the right way. *SAVED!*
Noooooooooooo!

It was all over and Italy, not England, were the Euro
2020 winners. While the Azzurri players raced away
to celebrate, Bukayo stood frozen in shock on the edge
of the six-yard box, with tears streaming down his face.
Why hadn't he placed his shot further in the corner? He
was usually so good at penalties!

Bukayo wasn't crying alone for long, though. One by
one, his England teammates raced over to console him:
Kalvin, then Luke, then Mason, Harry and Raheem…

'Don't worry, these things happen in football,' they
said, putting their arms around him. 'Lift your head up
high – you've been amazing, B!'

Southgate was the next to come over and comfort
him. 'Bukayo, it was my decision for you to take that
penalty and you were brave enough to step forward
when I asked you to,' the England manager told him.
'You should be so proud of yourself and everything
you've achieved. Don't worry, we'll be back!'

Bukayo spent the next few days at home with
his family, recovering and reflecting on his Euro

2020 experience. His manager was right; while his tournament had ended on a painful low, there had been so many highs along the way – the man of the match performance against the Czech Republic, the win over Germany, the assist against Denmark...

Eventually Bukayo felt ready to speak out, about the penalty miss but also the horrible racist abuse he, Marcus and Jadon had received on social media afterwards:

'My reaction post-match said it all, I was hurting so much and I felt like I'd let you all and my England family down, but I can promise you this... I will not let that moment or the negativity that I've received this week break me.'

CHAPTER 22

BOUNCING BACK ON HIS BIRTHDAY!

5 September 2021, Wembley Stadium

It took time for Bukayo to fully recover from his Euro 2020 disappointment. England had got so close to glory, and he had given his all to help his team. Now, however, they had to move on to their next challenge: qualifying for the World Cup in 2022.

Bukayo only played the last few minutes of England's first match, a 4–0 win over Hungary, but he was back in Southgate's starting line-up for the second against Andorra. They were playing at Wembley again for the first time since the Euro final, and the 67,000 fans gave the team a warm heroes' welcome. There were loud cheers for every England star, but especially for Bukayo.

It felt good to be back in action for his country, and on his twentieth birthday, Bukayo was looking to celebrate in style. Bukayo almost scored in the sixteenth minute, but his shot deflected off a defender's leg and flew just wide of the post.

'Oooooooooohhhh!' he gasped, throwing his hands to his mouth.

But Andorra couldn't keep out Bukayo for long. Two minutes later, he burst into the box again, and this time, he delivered a dangerous cross into the middle. A defender managed to head the ball clear, but only as far as Jesse, who fired a shot into the bottom corner. *1–0!*

Now that they had one goal, the fans expected their team to keep scoring, but midway through the second half, the score was still 1–0. Against Andorra? Come on, England! Eventually, Southgate brought on Mason and Jack in attack, and they combined to win a penalty, which Harry scored. *2–0!*

After that, the goals and the football began to flow.

On the right wing, Bukayo used his skill to escape from three opponents and then slid the ball over to Jesse on the left. From the edge of the box, he sent a shot swerving past the keeper. *3–0!*

'Thanks, B!' Jesse shouted as they celebrated together.

Right, Bukayo had a birthday assist, but what about a birthday goal to go with it? With five minutes to go, Trent Alexander-Arnold played a corner short to Jesse, who quickly turned and looked up. He was on a hat-trick, but instead of shooting, he crossed the ball in towards the birthday boy. Bukayo attacked it with a powerful leap and headed it down into the bottom corner. 4–0!

Goooooooooooooooooooaaaaaaaaaaaaaaaalllllllllllllll llllllllllll!!!!!!!!!!!!!!!!!!!!

Hurraaaaaaaaay!

Saka! Saka! Saka!

It was definitely the most popular goal of the afternoon, not only for the England supporters but also the players.

'Yessss, B!' cheered Tyrone.

'Happy Birthday, mate!' yelled Mason.

'Well, we couldn't let you go home goalless tonight, could we?!' laughed Jack.

Meanwhile, on the sidelines, the England manager stood there clapping with a big smile on his face. Southgate was delighted to see his brave young star bouncing back.

Scoring at Wembley in front of the fans and all his family really was the perfect birthday present for Bukayo. After thanking Jesse for the assist, he made a '2' and a '0' with his hands and held them up to the crowd.

HURRAAAAAAAAAY!

SAKA! SAKA! SAKA!

Listening to the England supporters chanting his name was a proud moment that Bukayo would never forget. Despite his penalty miss in the Euro final, they still loved him, and that meant so much to him.

As if all that wasn't enough, at the end of the game, there was one more gift waiting for Bukayo: the Player of the Match award.

'Thanks everyone for your messages today and to

everyone in the stadium for the special atmosphere,' he posted later on social media. 'I cannot ask for a better twentieth birthday!'

CHAPTER 23

NORTH LONDON
DERBY DELIGHT

26 September 2021, Emirates Stadium

Next, it was time for Bukayo to bounce back for
Arsenal, as well as England. In the first five games of
the new Premier League season, he hadn't got any
goals or assists, but hopefully that was all about to
change in his club's biggest game of the season: the
North London derby.

On the morning of the match, Bukayo and Emile
ate breakfast together and there was only one thing on
their minds:

'How fantastic would it feel to score against
Tottenham today?'

Growing up at the Hale End academy, they had watched lots of the big derby games live at the Emirates, dreaming of the day when they might be out there on the pitch playing for their favourite club. And now they were two of Arsenal's brightest stars! So far, Bukayo had appeared in three North London derbies for the first team, but his record didn't make for good reading: one win, two defeats, zero goals and zero assists.

'It's time for me to do something about that!' he told Emile with a confident smile.

Going into the game, Spurs sat six places higher in the Premier League table, but it didn't look that way in the first half as Arsenal's attackers tore them apart.

In the eleventh minute, Bukayo got the ball on the right wing and dribbled dangerously at Sergio Reguilón. The Tottenham left-back expected him to try and cut inside on his left foot, but with a silky stepover Bukayo shifted the ball onto his right and crossed it in towards the penalty spot.

And guess who got on the end of it? Yes, Emile! He knew where to be and he swept the ball first time past the keeper to send the Arsenal fans absolutely wild. *1–0!*

'Come onnnnn!' Emile roared, sliding towards the corner flag on his knees, and so did Bukayo right behind him. It was a goal they had scored so many times together at Hale End, but now they were heroes for the first team!

After that, it was Arsenal all the way. Auba played a one-two with Emile and then rolled a shot into the bottom corner. *2–0!*

North London was looking very red indeed! Two of Arsenal's front three had scored already; that only left Bukayo to go.

'Yes!' he cried out as Emile controlled the ball in the middle of the field a few minutes later. He was all alone on the right wing, with lots of space to attack. As soon as the pass arrived, Bukayo dribbled forwards towards the penalty area at top speed. What next?

'Shoot! Shoot!' the Arsenal fans urged.

No, first he unselfishly tried to curl the ball over to Auba on the left, but his pass was blocked by a defender. Fortunately, however, it bounced straight back to Bukayo, inside the Tottenham box.

'Shoot! Shoot!'

This time, he listened to the fans. With his right foot, Bukayo coolly guided the ball past the keeper and into the net. *3–0!*

Gooooooooooooooooooooaaaaaaaaaaaaaaaalllllllllllllll lllllllllll!!!!!!!!!!!!!!!!!!!!

Yesssssss, Bukayo had done it; he had scored his first North London derby goal, and the feeling was just as fantastic as he had imagined it would be! He slid across the grass and knelt there with his arms out wide, smiling and listening to 60,000 fans singing his new favourite song.

I like it, I like it, I like it, I like it
Woah, woah, here we go
Saka and Emile Smith Rowe!

Bukayo was enjoying himself so much that he even did a little dance with his teammates Gabriel Magalhães and Thomas Partey. What a wonderful Sunday afternoon it was turning out to be for Arsenal!

At last, it looked like Arteta's plan for the future was taking shape. Yes, the club had spent lots of money on signings, but at the heart of the new Arsenal were two amazing homegrown heroes: Emile and Bukayo.

Bukayo, the electric winger from Ealing was back to his best and all set for another exciting year, for club and country.

Read on for a sneak preview of
another brilliant football story by
Matt and Tom Oldfield. . .

LACAZETTE

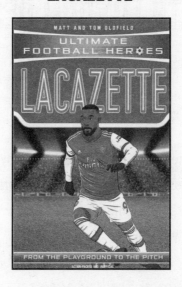

Available now!

CHAPTER 1

SAVING THE DAY IN THE NORTH LONDON DERBY

2 December 2018, Emirates Stadium

At half-time in the North London derby, things didn't look good for Arsenal. Their local rivals Tottenham were winning 2–1 and they weren't even playing that well.

Something had to change. Time for an Arsenal super sub, perhaps? That's what Alex was hoping as his teammates trudged into the dressing room. Because despite his exciting strike partnership with Pierre-Emerick Aubameyang, he was sat on the bench again.

Arsenal's manager Unai Emery had decided not to

start the two of them together in such a tough derby match, but Arsenal were losing – they needed 'Auba' *and* 'Laca' out there in attack!

Thankfully, by half-time, Emery had changed his mind. 'Alex and Aaron,' he called out. 'Get ready, you're coming on.'

Alex's eyes lit up – he would have the full second half to save the day! Although he much preferred playing from the start, he had a great record as a super sub – first in the France national youth teams when he was younger, and then at Arsenal. With his pace, power and skill, Alex could cause problems for any defence.

Plus, he loved big games, and derbies in particular. One of his favourite football memories was scoring a hat-trick for his hometown club Lyon against their local rivals, Saint-Étienne. Now, he had the chance to be Arsenal's derby hero too.

In the tunnel, Alex pulled his socks up and put his gloves on. Then he looked over at Pierre-Emerick.

'Let's win this!' he said with a very serious look on his face.

As Auba and Laca walked out together for the second half, the atmosphere in the stadium changed. Suddenly, the Arsenal supporters were hopeful again.

Come on, You Gunners!

Five minutes later, Aaron Ramsey raced forward from midfield and slipped the ball across to Pierre-Emerick, who curled a first-time shot into the back of the net.

Now Arsenal were level: 2–2 – game on! Arsenal attacked again and again, hunting for a winning goal. Sokratis missed a good chance, then Shkodran Mustafi, then Lucas Torreira. Oh dear – was the North London derby going to end in a disappointing draw?

No way, not while Alex was around! He tricked his way past Jan Vertonghen on the right wing and delivered a great cross towards Pierre-Emerick. It looked like a certain goal, but Juan Foyth got back just in time to head it away. Unlucky! Arsenal were getting closer and closer.

With fifteen minutes left, Aaron spotted Alex's run and played the perfect through-ball. On the edge of the penalty area, Alex paused to think. He had two defenders in front of him, and no-one to pass to. Oh well, he would just have to...

'Shoot!' the Arsenal fans urged. They knew how lethal their star striker could be.

BANG! Even though Alex struck it with his weaker left foot and slipped at the last second, his shooting accuracy was amazing. The ball skidded across the grass, past his old Lyon teammate Hugo Lloris, and into the bottom corner. *3–2!*

Goooooooooooooooooooaaaaaaaaaaaaaaaaaalllllllllllll llllllllllllll!!!!!!!!!!!!!!!!!!

The Emirates Stadium exploded with noise and excitement. On the touchline, Emery threw his arms up in the air – what a double substitution! Alex was usually a calm, quiet character, but not after scoring such an important goal. He sprinted away from his teammates and then slid towards the corner flag on his knees.

Pierre-Emerick was the first to catch up with him. 'Laca, I love you, man!' he screamed in Alex's ear.

As they got back up, they did their special

handshake together. With one arm behind their backs, they bowed at each other and then shook hands like old-fashioned gentlemen.

'Well done, sir!'

Alex had just saved the day for Arsenal in the North London derby. It was another unforgettable night for Lyon's favourite son.

Arsenal

🏆 FA Cup: 2019–20

🏆 Community Shield: 2020

Individual

🏆 Europa League Young Player of the Season: 2019–20

🏆 Arsenal Player of the Season: 2020–21

SAKA

(7) **THE FACTS**

NAME: Bukayo Ayoyinka Saka

DATE OF BIRTH: 5th September 2001

PLACE OF BIRTH: Ealing, London

NATIONALITY: English

BEST FRIEND: Emile Smith Rowe

CURRENT CLUB: Arsenal

POSITION: RW/LW/LB

THE STATS

Height (cm):	179
Club appearances:	126
Club goals:	22
Club assists:	27
Club trophies:	2
International appearances:	14
International goals:	4
International trophies:	0
Ballon d'Ors:	0

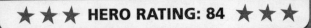

★ ★ ★ **HERO RATING: 84** ★ ★ ★

GREATEST MOMENTS

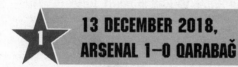

13 DECEMBER 2018,
ARSENAL 1–0 QARABAĞ

This Europa League match was Bukayo's first-ever start for Arsenal, and at the age of just seventeen, he was the best player on the pitch. From the left wing, he attacked with skill, speed and confidence, and although he narrowly missed scoring a goal, his very promising performance received much praise from players and pundits alike.

19 SEPTEMBER 2019, EINTRACHT FRANKFURT 0–3 ARSENAL

In the first game of the next Europa League season, Bukayo put on a real break-out performance. In between amazing assists for Joe Willock and Pierre-Emerick Aubameyang, he fired a dipping, swerving shot into the bottom corner to score his first senior goal for Arsenal. At the final whistle, as they walked around the pitch together arm in arm, Auba pointed at Bukayo, as if to say to the supporters, 'This guy is going to be great!'

1 AUGUST 2020, ARSENAL 2–1 CHELSEA

Although Bukayo stayed on the bench for this FA Cup final win, it was still a huge moment for him. He had played a key part in the earlier rounds with a goal and an assist, and he got to lift his first senior trophy at Wembley with three of his friends from the Arsenal academy: Joe, Reiss Nelson, and Eddie Nketiah.

22 JUNE 2021,
ENGLAND 1–0 CZECH REPUBLIC

Bukayo was a surprise starter in England's third group game at Euro 2020, but he was absolutely brilliant, winning the Man of the Match award. Although he didn't get the goal or assist, he played a crucial part in England's victory with his bursting runs up the right wing. It was the beginning of a huge tournament for Bukayo.

26 SEPTEMBER 2021,
ARSENAL 3–1 TOTTENHAM

After a slow start to the new Premier League season, this was the day Bukayo got back to his electric best. In his fourth North London derby, he was the star of the show, scoring one goal and setting up another for his old friend Emile Smith Rowe. From the Hale End academy, Bukayo and Emile had risen up to become Arsenal's brightest stars.

PLAY LIKE YOUR HEROES

RACING UP THE RIGHT WING
LIKE BUKAYO SAKA

STEP 1: As a winger, your main job is to attack, but don't forget to also track back and do your defensive work as well.

STEP 2: Then, once your team has possession, ZOOM! – up the pitch you go, racing into space on the right wing to receive a pass.

STEP 3: When the ball arrives, don't be afraid to go forward. Use your speed and skill to dribble at the defender in front of you, daring them to try and tackle you.

STEP 4: As you run with the ball, keep your head up and stay aware of the teammates around you. If a pass is on, play it. If not, carry on attacking!

STEP 5: When a defender eventually closes you down, it's time to make a quick decision. You're famous for your powerful left foot, so try to cut inside and shoot if you can.

STEP 6: But if that option's blocked, remember that your right foot is really good too. With a stylish stepover, shift the ball across and BANG!

STEP 7: GOAL! Make sure to celebrate with all your teammates like the humble hero you are.